#12 OF OUR SHORT BOOKS YOU'LL ACTUALLY READ

Boost

YOUR VEHICLE TO WORK FROM ANYWHERE, BE WELL, & LIVE THE LIFE OF YOUR DREAMS

ANDREW EDWIN JENKINS

W/ ERNIE YARBROUGH

 **+** A BOOK YOU'LL ACTUALLY READ ABOUT TIME + MONEY FREEDOM

Boost. Copyright 2020, Andrew Edwin Jenkins.

ISBN number = 9798634996714

#12 in the series of OilyApp+ Books You'll Actually Read

For more info about this title, video content, and more, go to www.OilyApp.com/Boost (URL is case-sensitive).

Connect online!

Podcast-
OilyApp.com

Social-
www.Facebook.com/OilyApp
www.Facebook.com/OilyApp
www.Instagram.com/OilyApp

YouTube-
www.YouTube.com/OilyApp

Website-
OilyApp.com

Contents

What to Expect This Time   5

Part 1 = Life is Too Short

1. Time for a Do-Over   11
2. The Villain = The Time for Money Tango   27
3. Mindset Shift   43
4. Breaking Through the Glass Ceiling (Finally)   63
5. "Normal" People Doing Real Life   85

Part 2 = Three Secrets *They* Don't Want You to Know

6. Secret #1 = You Must Own + Invest to Get Ahead   97
7. Secret #2 = You Can Earn While You Learn   109
8. Secret #3 = You Can Do It Without Selling Stuff…   125

Part 3 = The Real Question

9. If / Then   151

10. This *Might Be* Your Jetpack   161

11. Your Next Step   173

12. Links + Resources   177

What to Expect This Time

We created OilyApp (go to OilyApp.com to learn more) with the goal of educating you about Young Living's vast array of incredible products. The app is uniquely the *only* third party app that's an approved partner of Young Living Essential Oils, passing a strict compliance review each time we update.

OilyApp works well with Young Living's stated mission of taking oils into every home in the world. Once people have the oils, *they need to know how to use them*.

Whereas shipping a desk reference to everyone is cumbersome and difficult (besides, who wants to always lug it around!?), most people have a smart phone. An app is the perfect solution.

Furthermore, our app does other things a book can't do. When Young Living releases a new product, we don't do a reprint– we simply push a notification to people who paid the one-time fee to purchase the app. And, you can manage your personal inventory, create wish lists, watch videos, and access other training tools, as well- all impossibilities with a book.

(I know, the total irony of reading all of that in a book isn't lost on me.)

Furthermore, the app was created by actual members (Ernie and his wife, Myra, are Royal Crown Diamonds, the highest rank in the company). In other words, our founder created the app in the field for use in the field.

The next thing + how *Boost* fits

After a few years of providing users with OilyApp, it became apparent that another addition was needed for product users and business builders who wanted to go to the "next level." Enter OilyApp+, a web-based experience designed to provide users with more relevant information– things like scripts they could use to learn and/or educate their teams, graphics that were relevant and educational, and videos that provide deep-dive training.

We created OilyApp+ in less than two weeks from its conception.

From the beginning, we knew we wanted the OA+ to include video courses and online scripts– tools you could use to review and then teach your "people" what you were learning.

After a few weeks, the thought hit us: *What if we made the scripts into small books, too– small pocket-sized books people could easily review and use to study, to lead others, and even to teach classes?*

Hence the title you have in your hand, #12 in our series. **This book is unique because it is not written to teach you about the products specifically. Rather, it's written to explain *why* you should seriously consider Young Living as a viable business**.

In this book you'll learn the following:

- If you're like most people, you're not financially where you want to be (chapter 1).

- The thing that keeps you trapped is the time-for-money swap– that's our villain (chapter 2).

- You probably have some reservations about network marketing, but this way of doing business– though not perfect– is better, and it actually fits nicely with emerging global and economic trends (chapter 3).

- Normal people– folks like you and me– can do this, getting great results (chapters 4 & 5).

- The key to financial freedom is to move away from being "Employee" (even a "Self-Employed" employee) and become a Business Owner + Investor, but there are so many roadblocks that this seems impossible (in chapter 6 I'll show you how to do it with the same amount of money you spent at Starbucks last month).

- You probably don't have the ability to leave your current income stream to obtain training for a new one and then get that business off the ground, so we'll outline a way to "learn while you earn," even while you maintain your current obligations (chapter 7).

- You can do this without become the person people try to avoid, because you're always pushing a product (in chapter 8 we'll discover that people will actually seek your help).

- Finally, I'll provide you with a grid whereby you can decide if this is an opportunity worthy of your pursuit (chapters 9 & 10).

My assessment… is that, yes, it's worth the time it takes to investigate all of this info and then implement this strategy.

(I understand, too, that you might be reading this book and *not* be a member of Young Living– someone might have offered this to you as an invitation to explore and learn more.)

Your family is worth it, your dreams are worth it, and life is simply too valuable to find yourself stuck doing something you won't want to be doing so you can simply make it through another week, keeping food on the table, gas in the tank, and power on at the house.

Oh, and in the middle of this book, I've got a treat. The founder of OilyApp, Ernie Yarbrough, is going to pull back the curtain and tell you a bit of his story in chapter 5. Unless you're told otherwise in the pages that follow, assume I'm the one writing and "speaking" with you.

All the best,

Andy

April 2020

Part 1 = Life is Too Short

1. Time for a Do-Over

About a year ago I ran into a friend from high school, Jason, at Starbucks.

"What are you up to?" he asked.

"What do you mean?"

I knew he could have been asking that question in one of two ways:

- On one hand, he might have meant, "What are you doing right now, this precise second?"

- On the other, he might have been asking a "bigger picture" type of question, such as, "How's life been treating you?"

"Today," he said. "You look like you've got a pile of things in your hand. What are you about to do?"

Whew, I thought. *I'm off the hook*.

As I gathered my wits, contemplating how I would have answered the *second* version of that question in light of the poop-storm the previous 2-plus years had been, I answered him. **"I'm working on an online course and a book to offer people hope, to outline a way they can become financially free… that they can live and work from anywhere, they can pursue the life of their dreams, they can do more good than they ever imagined possible, and they can bring others along with them on that journey."**

"Interesting," he replied. "Tell me more."

As I thought back to the previous 24 months, that sequence of events I *didn't* want to tell him, I offered, "I just thought I would be in a different place in life right now. And, though I can't change *some* things– like how others treat me, and how others react amidst some really difficult life-situations– I can *certainly* change other things, like how attached I am to the rat race and how much time I have to focus on the things that truly matter. I'm working on a tool that will help people break free from that. At least *that* will be one less source of drama in life."

After a few moments, he offered, "I need to see it. I think I could actually use something different. I need a second chance myself, a do-over."

In his mid-40s, Jason is what you would label *successful*. Has a wife and a solid marriage. Three kids. Nice house. Two cars. He's nice-looking and has been physically fit since high school. Has a job as a pharmaceutical sales rep. His wife can stay home with the kids if she wants– they make plenty of money. Yet he wanted a do-over. He doesn't look *anything* like someone who needs another chance at life.

Never judge a book by the cover, right?

"What do you mean?" I asked.

Then, after a pause and a puff of emotional release, the answer. "I'm just keeping my head above water. It's too much. I like what I do, but it's too much."

"Really?"

I (wrongly) assumed that what I was writing– and creating– was only for people who *didn't* seem to have it together, people who *looked* like they needed money, people whose financial outlook was hurtling towards the ground at Mach-1. Those are the people (in my mind) who need a parachute– anything that might be their lucky break.

"Yeah. We're doing alright financially, but I never see the family. My oldest boy is graduating high school, and it's suddenly hit me that the others are on the way out the door, right behind him."

"So you want to make some adjustments?"

"Yeah, I do."

"That's what I'm writing about," I said.

I explained I was beginning to realize *a lot* of people find themselves mid-life (that's what he and I officially are now, mid-life-ers) and wish they could to back, reboot, and do things in a different way.

I continued, "Sometimes, a crisis forces us there. A spouse leaves and we're left picking up the pieces of what we once thought was something beautiful that we were building together…"

(That was my story– *is my story*. After 20 years, she called it quits.)

"Other times," he suggested, "we just sense it. We feel it. Our intuition just tells us that that's something different for us, something *more*."

Then, I added, "Or we just find that we're tired. Exhausted. There too much month left at the end of the money, too many things to do but not enough day to do them…"

"And those days," he interjected, "seem incredibly long, yet the weeks just fly by and seem so short."

"And yet we have nothing to show for it," I concluded. "You do all of this work and all of this responsible *adulting*, as they call it, but there's no net gain…"

"I get it," Jason replied. "I'm somewhere in the middle of all of that– minus the crisis part."

I wanted to explain to him that I was actually smack dab in the middle of that crisis scenario, but yet I didn't want to. Like him, there was more to *my story* than what anyone walking into that coffee shop might have seen that day.

"Regardless of how people find themselves there," I offered, "and there's usually not a single answer, I lot of people want that do-over– that second-shot at life."

It could be different, though...

I continued, "That's one of the things we do. **We help people get a new start, another starting line, another way to move forward from where they are to where they've always dreamed– or might have even been afraid to dream– they could be**."

"Tell me more," he said– it was the second time he encouraged me to do so within the ten minutes we had been chatting.

So, I did. I spoke to him about our dreams, our failures, our fears, our suspicions, and that nagging feeling we all have that we've just been held back by some invisible force that works against us.

Jason and I discussed five reasons many of us feel we're not where we want to be. I'm not saying this is the "end all" definitive discussion on the matter. I'm just saying **these are the five we talked about...**

1. The dreams we have deserve time + space to be pursued, but we're in a time crunch

2. Our past failures *shouldn't* disqualify us from our true potential

3. Our fear of *not* trying should be greater than our fear of failing

4. The current system is set up to enslave– not empower

5. If often feels like we're held back— not helped up

1. The dreams we have deserve time + space to be pursued

The two of us agreed that we both wanted something *more*. Life simultaneously felt full and a bit hollow at the same time.

When we graduate high school, we anticipate working somewhere doing something meaningful and exciting. We "sign up" to make a difference. We don't sign up for 40 years of 40 hours of grind.

YOU HAVE A HUNCH THAT LIFE COULD BE BETTER, THAT THERE'S "MORE" OUT THERE, THAT PERHAPS YOU COULD CHANGE THE WORLD IN SOME WAY...

WE'LL SHOW YOU HOW TO DO THAT IN THIS BOOK

Besides that, many people find themselves taking work home with them just to keep from getting behind. Our mobile phones stay attached to our hips (in case something "important" happens), and we routinely check our email before exiting our beds in the morning. Some of us *not only* do this at our full-time job, *but also* at second and third places of employment.

Some of us dream life could be better, we dream we could help others along the way, or we dream we could have more time to share with the people who matter the most to us. But, our time is already crunched.

When would something new fit in– and where's the on-ramp?

2. Our past failures *shouldn't* disqualify us from our true potential

The first time I attended an "award trip" from the network marketing company whose products I promote, I assumed I would be "out-classed" by the other distributors who were there. That doesn't mean I thought they were more important than me (even though I did have some serious insecurity issues)– we're all created equal. Rather, I thought they had some skillset or some extraordinary life experience that qualified them to achieve something I couldn't do.

I was wrong.

The first guy I met explained to me that, before they found this business opportunity, they lived paycheck-to-paycheck.

"I mean, we were tight," he said. Then– "I just bought a new car. On my old one the windshield wipers didn't work–- nor did the air conditioner. When it rained, we had to stick our head out the window to be able to see. If it was during the summer that meant we got hot and wet. If it was during the winter we got cold and wet. It was miserable."

Less than 90 days from that convo, he and his wife hit the top rank in the company.

Another guy I met described how a church used to bring them boxes of food. A super-tough chapter in life meant he lost his house, almost lost his job, and had six figures of medical bills piling up.

Yet another man detailed the stupid series of business decisions which led to he and his wife *losing* their first "brick and mortar" business.

"We watched the landlord come carry our furniture out– and all of our merchandise– as collateral for back rent. Our little girls had no clue what was happening. They just sat the on the floor at the side of the store, eating their sandwiches."

These three men– and their wives– were all at the top ranks in the company. And they'd only been working the new business for less than two years. In other words, **nothing in their past experience would have even hinted that they could *ever* reach the level of success they currently enjoyed**– much less do it so quickly.

They had all failed– in drastic ways.

That's good news for you and me. You see, we don't have to lean on our unique skillset in order to make this business successful. We can simply work the system, taking the specific steps outlined in the training materials.

And, though our results may vary, the top levels of the company are filled with people who have bankruptcies, foreclosures, divorces, and failed businesses in their past.

A mentor once told me, "Don't trust someone who doesn't walk with a limp."

That is, "Don't listen to someone who hasn't failed– and who isn't honest about their failures."

You see, the truth is that we all have clutter in our pasts. *All* of us.

Anyone who suggests they don't… is lying. And, **anyone who can't be honest about the tough stuff of life isn't being honest about the best stuff in life, either**.

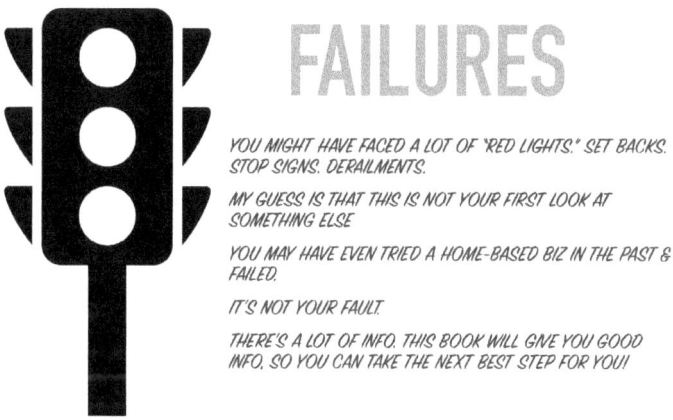

FAILURES

YOU MIGHT HAVE FACED A LOT OF "RED LIGHTS." SET BACKS. STOP SIGNS. DERAILMENTS.

MY GUESS IS THAT THIS IS NOT YOUR FIRST LOOK AT SOMETHING ELSE

YOU MAY HAVE EVEN TRIED A HOME-BASED BIZ IN THE PAST & FAILED.

IT'S NOT YOUR FAULT.

THERE'S A LOT OF INFO. THIS BOOK WILL GIVE YOU GOOD INFO, SO YOU CAN TAKE THE NEXT BEST STEP FOR YOU!

You might have actually tried network marketing (sometimes referred to as multi-level marketing) in the past. You might have even failed. A lot of the people I met at the first trip had, too.

Let me say this clearly: even if you failed in the past, it's not your fault. There are great ways to run a home business and there are… well… ways that don't work. In this book I'll outline a few things that will let you know if this is something that might work for you, so you'll know the next best step to take for you and your family. Whatever you decide, though, **your past is not a predictor of your true potential.** In fact, past failures can become springboards to future success if you're willing to be honest about them, learn from them, and then avoid letting them define you.

3. Our fear of *not* trying should be greater than our fear of failing

Some people are afraid of trying something new– and fear that this opportunity might not work for them.

First of all, let me say this: **it's OK to be afraid of new things**.

Lately, there's a mantra going around (on the Internet and even in some popular songs) that says, "Fear is a liar."

Ummm… *nope*. I don't think so.

Fear is an honest emotion. And, it's actually *healthy* to be afraid of *some* things.

Think about it. Your fear keeps you from walking down a dark alley alone, your fear tells you not to step too close to the edge of a cliff, and your fear cautions you that some people might not have your best interest at heart.

In other words, fear can actually serve you.

Now, we don't want to be *controlled* by fear, but we do want to listen to it. And, we want to hear what it's saying.

My hunch is this, though. **You're probably more afraid of things staying "status quo" than you are seeing something change for the good**.

At the same time, you might be a smidge afraid that this opportunity won't work for you…

- Maybe you're afraid that you're too old (or young)
- Maybe you're afraid that you don't know enough people
- Maybe you're afraid that you'll have to invest a lot of time + money into learning something new

Over the next few pages, I'll put all of those fears to rest.

MAYBE YOU'RE CONCERNED THAT YOU "CAN'T DO IT."

LET ME PUT YOUR FEARS TO REST. WE HAVE A SYSTEM…

YOU JUST NEED SOMEONE TO EXPLAIN IT TO YOU…

IT'S WORKED FOR OTHERS. IT WILL WORK FOR YOU, TOO!

We have a proven system. It works for young people (and old), it works for educated people (and uneducated people), it works for men (and women), it works if you're an introvert (or extrovert), it works if you know a lot of people (or if you don't know many people at all). Our system has worked for others, and it will work for you with the same effectiveness. You just need someone to explain it to you.

4. The current system is set up to enslave— not empower

Now, the last few paragraphs may have just gone against *everything* you've been taught. The truth is that big corporations, banks, and schools want you to *think* you need a college degree, a stack of start-up money, a lengthy resume, and a list of contacts in order to start something substantial and long-lasting. They all have their own reasons for wanting you to think that, but it's not true.

BIG CORPORATIONS, SCHOOLS, BANKS, AND EVEN SOME OF THE PEOPLE YOU KNOW WHAT YOU TO THINK THAT YOU NEED A DEGREE AND A LOT OF START-UP $$$ TO BUILD SOMETHING...

THEY ALL HAVE THEIR REASONS FOR WANTING YOU TO THINK THAT, BUT IT'S JUST NOT TRUE...

After reading chapter 3, you'll understand why they want you to think that way.

5. Held back or helped up?

Again, if you think corporations, banks, the healthcare industry, and others don't want you to succeed… you're probably (to some degree) right. They don't benefit from you stepping off the treadmill and creating your own path.

HELD BACK?

AGAIN, IF YOU THOUGHT "THE SYSTEM" DIDN'T WANT YOU TO SUCCEED... WHETHER IT'S BIG CORPORATIONS, THE HEALTHCARE INDUSTRY... THE EDUCATION SYSTEM... THERE'S PROBABLY SOME TRUTH TO THAT.

THEY DON'T BENEFIT FROM YOU SUCCEEDING.

THE DIFFERENCE? WE CARE ABOUT YOUR AND YOUR FREEDOM... AND TRULY WANT YOU TO LIVE THE LIFE OF YOUR DREAMS.

THE BIGGEST BATTLE... WILL BE THE ONE BETWEEN YOUR EARS. THE WAR IN YOUR MIND.

The difference is that we care about your freedom…and truly want you to live the life of your dreams.

Plus, as you'll discover later in the book, we only succeed when we help you succeed. (Wait until you read my "ah-ha" moment in point 5 of chapter 4.)

The result

Let me be clear about the journey we're going to take over the next few pages. That way, when you get to the end of this short book you'll be able to look back and say, "Ahh, yes… I can see it. This makes sense." Then, you can decide the next best step for you.

First, I'm going to show you a business vehicle that will do the following:

- Encourage you to walk into the identity of the leader you really are (even if you don't consider yourself a leader).

- Equip you with a business system that has a proven track record (in other words, it's worked for others so you can verify that it will also work for you).

- Empower you to help others in ways you never dreamed possible.

- Effectively unite people towards a common mission– even as you work for yourself. (Rising tides float everyone's boat a little bit higher, so we'll discover ways to raise the water level together.)

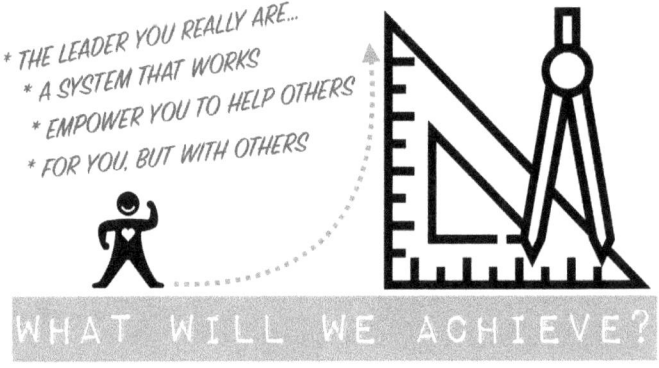

Second, this business vehicle will provide you the opportunity to work from anywhere and live the life of your dreams– all while you:

- Escape the 9-5

- Live well (physically, financially, emotionally, relationally)

- Do more good (leave a positive mark everywhere you go)

- Bring other people on the journey with you

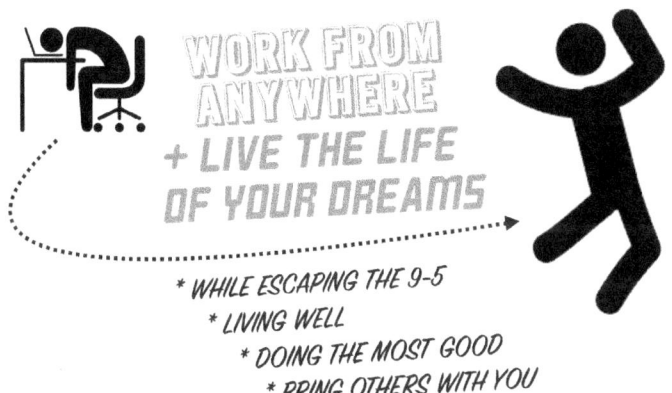

Furthermore, I'll show you how we can achieve all of this even if you don't have a lot of time or money to begin. If you find yourself in the same position as most people, you probably *don't* have a lot of extra time or money (which may be your reason for reading this book). Speaking of those two issues– time and money– let's roll right into the next chapter where we'll discuss how the time-for-money tango really is the chief enemy of our freedom.

1. TIME FOR A DO-OVER

2. The Villain – The Time for Money Tango

Think back to how people used to travel– back when people *only* had horses…

At some point, somebody somewhere had the bright idea, "Let's add a cart to the horse, let the horse pull it, and toss all of our things on it. Then, we won't have to carry *anything*."

Hence, the first horse-and-carriage configuration was born.

Not too long after that someone else thought, "Gee, I bet this thing would move a lot faster if we tied *two* horses together and let them pull that big wagon…"

Alas, it worked. Before long, people regularly lassoed three and four– or even more – horses together. The wagons grew bigger while, at the same time, the speed of forward progress got faster.

There's no way things could ever improve. Or, so people thought.

A better version of the old or something entirely different altogether?

Henry Ford famously quipped, "If you asked people what they wanted, they would have said, 'A faster carriage.'"

That is, "String more horses together and figure out a way to move them *even quicker.*"

But that's not what they needed. **Even though that's all they could envision in their minds, they needed something *quantum-leap-like* in order to continue moving forward.** Strapping more horses together and creating bigger wagons, at some point, would prove too cumbersome and too costly. They needed something… *uniquely different.*

Enter the Model T, the car you could get in any color you wanted… according to Ford himself, "As long as it's black."

(I know, color is another monumental leap altogether, showing that even exponential jumps themselves aren't exempt from constant improvement.)

The first automobile offered people a totally new grid whereby they could understand transportation. If adding another horse to a wagon, or making a bigger wagon, was the equivalent of 1 + 2 + 3 + 4 + 5 with each new improvement made, moving from animal energy to mechanical energy was like shifting from addition to multiplication. That is, it was like going to 1 x 2 x 3 x 4 x 5 with each adjustment.

Do the math.

- 1 + 2 + 3 + 4 + 5 = 15
- 1 x 2 x 3 x 4 x 5 = 120

That's a big difference in output– particularly in such a radically short amount of time.

The Model T wasn't just a speedier option. Nor was it simply cleaner (no more poop to shovel in the middle of the road). Nor was it merely more efficient (fuel one car rather than feeding multiple mouths). It was an entire *shift*, a totally new way of living.

Another pair of shoes or a jetpack?

Look at the title of this book, *Boost*. I contemplated naming the book something different, but I couldn't think of a better analogy between where many of us are and where need to be– vocationally– than the comparison between a pair of shoes and a jetpack.

Over the past 30 years athletic shoes have improved a lot.

I began playing basketball, back in the 4th grade, in a pair of Nike Cortez low-tops. Mine were white leather with a red leather swoosh. At the time, the only other option was a blue leather swoosh (which my little brother chose) or a "natural" swoosh (read: white suede).

A few years later, Nike introduced the first Air Jordan shoes. They appeared to be a magnificent leap forward. No longer were you stuck with white shoes; these came in black and red. And, they had two criss-crossed laces– one red and the other black.

Converse countered. They released purple and yellow hi-tops (to match Magic Johnson's Lakers uniform), as well green "All Stars" to couple with Larry Byrd's green Celtics outfit. Athletic shoes were progressing.

In time, every pro athletic team had stripes and swooshes to match their uniforms. Teams were no longer tied to "basic black" or "totally white." They had options.

But, at the end of the day, those were just the same shoes with different colors. It was the equivalent of *painting a horse*. Yes, you read that right. Most sneaker improvements, in the grand scheme, were the equivalent of brushing liquid latex on an animal.

Even the advent of visible Nike Air soles (the clear cushions you could actually *see* and squish with your fingers) and Reebok Pumps (you literally squeezed a basketball-shaped inflator on the tongue of the shoes) all proved nothing more than incremental changes to the original sneakers.

In fact, the recent "throwback" to the original shoes, coupled with zero-drop designs all demonstrate that, as far as sneakers go, we're still doing the $1 + 2 + 3 + 4 + 5$ game. And, sometimes, we do $5 + 4 + 3 + 2 + 1$. That is, we're still progressing– and even regressing– by addition.

If you're going to move faster, then, you can't just– hypothetically speaking– get a pair of lighter, better colored, or more gizmo'd sneakers. You need something totally different.

You need a jetpack.

I know. Moving from sneakers to a jetpack doesn't seem fair. It's like introducing a completely different variable into the mix.

But that's exactly what's needed. **A big life-leap doesn't require *just* more efficiency. Or even *just* better design. Your jump requires something totally new, something *categorically different*.**

Face it. Escaping the 9-5, working from anywhere, and living the life of your dreams isn't possible with a mere shoe upgrade. You've been there, done it, and have the merit badge. You've invested the effort; you've done the time. If it was going to happen with mere incremental changes, it would have *already* come to fruition. You would have *already* seen results.

(And, as many of us get older, the truth is that we all sense we're running out of time to do the things which matter the most.)

No, nothing will change unless something radically changes.

You need a jetpack. Not a new pair of shoes (not even those "heelies"– the tennis shoes that had hidden wheels inside the soles which I purchased for my kids a few years ago). A bonafide jetpack.

All that said, here's what I'll *begin* showing you in this chapter (and what I'm going to try to prove to you in the rest of this book):

1. **The best way to change your financial outlook is by becoming a network marketing professional.** Yes, there are other ways to do it– and people do it all the time. This isn't the only way, but this is the *best* way.

2. **The best way to "do" network marketing is with Young Living Essential Oils**, the company I've joined (again, there are

other ways to do network marketing, but my biased opinion is that this is the *best* way).

In other words, that 1-2 punch is your jetpack. It is your opportunity to hang up the running shoes (particularly if you're stuck on the rat-race hamster wheel) and strap on your personal jetpack.

Your arch-enemy = time / money swap

The biggest obstacle to moving forward– **the thing that keeps us moving fast all day while making minimal forward progress towards our dreams– is the time-for-money-tango** (make note: we're way busier than ever, but with far less to show for it).

Or, to say it another way, *the time-for-money swap is your enemy.*

That means this:

- **You give time; you get money in return.** Five days a week, you offer your time to an employer in exchange for some money. You give them eight hours a day, and then remit you with 40 hours of pay.

It also works like this:

- **You *don't* give time; you *don't* get money.** If you don't give away that eight hours a day, then they don't give you those 40 hours of pay.

Our basic assumption– and the reality most of us live– is this: you can't have both. That is, you *must* exchange time for money. And, the more you have of one, the less you have of the other.

When I was in college, I worked 15-20 hours per week at a local department store selling shoes. In general, I worked two nights a week (for four hours) and at least on day on the weekend (for 8 or 9 hours). During that phase of my life, I had very few responsibilities outside of my schooling. Therefore, I had a lot of time– so much so that I often found myself *bored*.

But I didn't have much money.

When I enrolled in seminary and began pursuing my Master's degree, I found myself taking class with a lot of students my age, as well as several that were 20 and 30 years older. Whereas I earned a 3.5 year graduate school degree in 2 years, many of my older classmates were on a 9-10 year plan. Whereas I doubled-up on classes, the older students took about 20% of a full-time load.

I didn't have much money during that season, but I had plenty of time to take extra classes. Those older classmates, on the other hand, juggled families and full-time careers, often leading churches or spearheading nonprofits. They didn't have much time– they had to spend their non-class hours earning money in order to take care of their families and handle their other responsibilities.

My experience and theirs confirm what many of us believe: **when you're in the rat race, the more free time we have, the less money we have. The more money we have (or, the more money require– even for things like house payments, utility bills and groceries), the less time we have**.

I've learned, though, that this time-for-money swap is a false dichotomy that we've been conditioned to live under.

Untangle the lie

Let's take a closer look at what this swap means. I promise, this thought process is so embedded in how we do things that most of us move through the week on auto-pilot without even thinking about it.

Think back to my classmates. Some of them were 40 or 50. That seemed so... *old*... back then.

They didn't have much time to take classes, because their work schedules required them to "spend" that time somewhere else– namely, their jobs. In the same way that money is the currency for the transfer of goods and commodities (i.e., food and gas and the other things we all need), **time is most commonly the currency of exchange for money**.

I had "free" time– and plenty of it. I wasn't spending my time to earn money.

My position looked like this:

They, on other hand, had much more money than I did. They were buying houses, financing cars, and paying for braces and other things their kids needed. They had money, but not much time.

Their predicament looked more like this:

You've probably found yourself in the same position— on both sides of the equation. Think about it…

- If you (or your kids) are sick and you need to take the day off from work, you lose a day's pay– unless you have "sick time" available.

- If you're self-employed and you go on vacation, you lose the money you would have earned had you traded your time for that money rather than keeping that time for yourself.

Most people make this swap every day, the general consensus being that time occupies one side of a scale and money occupies the other.

We'd love to find the right balance, because we all know that when one goes up, the other goes down.

Look at the graphic above.

This is such a pervasive mindset that I've dedicated an entire chapter of this book (chapter 6, "Secret #1 = You Must Own + Invest to Get Ahead") to show you what economists and successful business leaders have said about this villain and how you can break free from it.

Even if not motivated by money...

For about 12 months I attended a men's small group. We met every Thursday morning at 7am for coffee, opened up the Bible, and got raw about life. By 8am, each of the guys hit the door, cranked their cars, and sped off to work.

One day the youngest guy in the group, Ty, asked me, "What do you do? You're never rushing out like the rest of us."

I vaguely explained that I worked from home and had a few projects going, things that required time but didn't keep my tied to a specific location at a specific hour on the clock. And, because of that, I was able to leverage some things…

"It all enables me to work from anywhere, manage some things on my own schedule, and take advantage of some opportunities I never imagined I would have."

"Would it work for me?" he asked, making him the second person in about three weeks who approached me about a life-change due to a lack of margin in their calendar.

I told him it would– "If you're coachable. I mean, if you can look at the system and follow the instructions, and if you're willing to learn while you earn."

"I can probably do that," he said. Then– "I mean, I have to do that all day where I'm working at right now, right?"

As we laughed, he hit me with a follow-up question.

"I'd like to escape this grind," he said, "but I'm not motivated by money."

"What do you mean?" I asked.

"I mean that… well… a lot of people want to make $100,000 a year. I don't. I don't want a fancy car or a huge house or any of that stuff. I just want to provide for my family. The problem is that I have to work 60-70 hours a week to do it."

"Think about what you just said," I offered. "You told me you work 60-70 hours most weeks…"

"Yeah. *Easily*. Sometimes even more."

"Why?"

"Because I have bills. And two small kids. And my wife is pregnant with another one on the way."

"And what do the bills and the groceries and the diapers and everything else require?"

"Money," he said. "They all require money."

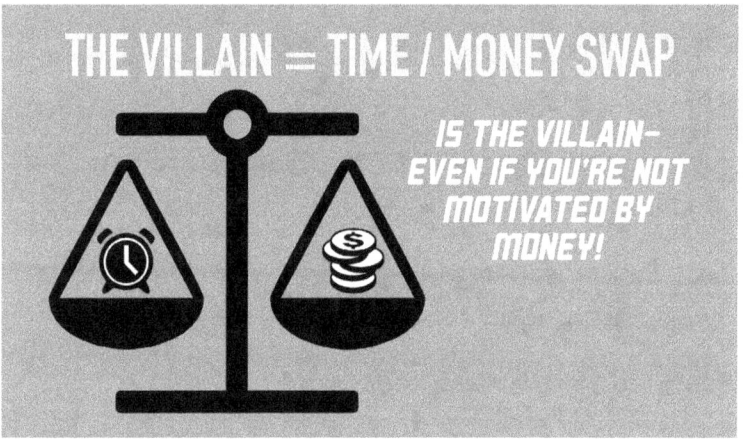

"There's your answer," I replied. "**Pursuing a new opportunity doesn't have to be motivated by a desire to be rich. In fact, for most people it's not. It's about freedom– and that's the one thing that you don't currently have.** Right now, you're giving your employer those 70 hours and he's giving you money. If you work less, you have more time…"

"… but I won't have as much money as a I need for our bills if I cut back my hours. I've tried it."

"Right. Yet when you hit the sweet spot with the amount of money you need to keep things floating…"

"… then I don't have any time with my family."

"Bingo. You need a different vehicle. You're still driving a horse and carriage. You'd probably settle for a car… but what you really need is a jetpack."

But what if you could have both?

After a few moments Ty asked me, as if scratching his head, "You still work, don't you?"

"Yeah," I chuckled. "I still do. In fact, I work hard. The key, though, is that I work on my schedule. And, due to the business model that we work with, I leverage my work with the work of hundreds and even thousands of others. It means you get a better result with a lot less lifting."

"I'd have to change a lot of things," he said.

"Not really. In fact, **most people can make a few minor shifts- the majority of those changes being mental adjustments- and see some degree of success fairly quickly. Then rather than chasing time or money, you'll see that both actually come to you.**"

"*To* you?"

"Yes. You'll still work. Some people enroll in a network marketing opportunity and think they can work *some* time (whenever they feel like it) or *eventual* time (whenever they decide to finally get around to it). You can't do that. Remember the premise of the book I'm putting together…"

(I was in the middle of writing the notes for this book when I met with Ty at the coffee shop to discuss this opportunity in detail.)

"Yeah," he said, "You said you can live and work from anywhere, escaping the 9-5… be well, and live the life of your dreams…"

He'd memorized the short script in just a few minutes.

"That's part of it. You *work* from anywhere. But you can work amidst the chaos and wonder of everyday life. The shift has given me the chance to write books, to travel, to homeschool my kids, to renovate my house during the workweek…"

"You're saying I have to be *consistent*."

"That's right," I confirmed. "**I'm not offering you a hall pass that enables you to live for *free*. Rather, I'm showing you a vehicle that will empower you to realize your dreams and live a life of *freedom*.**"

Then, I outlined the two statements I made earlier in this chapter, something I'll continue showing you throughout this book:

1. **The *best* way to change your financial outlook is by becoming a network marketing professional.** Yes, there are other ways to do it– and people do it all the time. This isn't the only way, but this is the *best* way.

2. **The *best* way to "do" network marketing is with Young Living Essential Oils**, the company I've joined (again, there are other ways to do network marketing, but my biased opinion is that this is the *best* way).

2. THE VILLAIN = THE TIME FOR MONEY TANGO

3. Mindset Shift

That day when I met Ty at the coffee shop, I told him that I wasn't offering a scenario whereby he could live for *free*. Rather, I was proposing that he could live a life of *freedom*. Notice the difference.

Furthermore, I suggested that it requires a few mental shifts in order to break away from the time-for-money paradigm that's been hardwired into us. In this chapter I'll outline four mental shifts you must make in order to make the transition work for you.

1. You must be open to earning residual income using a duplicatable model

2. You must to be willing to take an honest look at network marketing as a viable business model

3. You must be willing to *not* sell a bunch of stuff…

4. You must take note of the global economic trends– and be willing to work with them rather than against them

3. MINDSET SHIFT

These are each important, because **in order to fulfill our goal of living and working from anywhere in the manner outlined in this book, we've got to get onboard with all four of these**. Each provides fuel for your jetpack– the jetpack being your vehicle to move from where you are to where you want to be.

1. You must be open to earning residual income using a duplicatable model

The first mindset shift is easy to understand, but a lot of people have trouble finding a way to actually *do it*. So, let me explain how residual income works, by comparing and contrasting a few real-life business scenarios.

Scenario #1 = my grass cutting days.

I cut grass to earn money when I was in high school. The upside was that I made good money (for a high schooler) in a short amount of time. I could cut grass for the three months I was out of class for the summer and then have enough cash to fund me for *the entire school year*.

The downside was obvious: *if I didn't work, I didn't get paid*. If at any time I quit– even for a week or so to go on vacation with my family– *the money simply stopped coming*.

Don't get be wrong, cutting grass was– and is– a great job. It's good because you can do it over and over and over again. The grass keeps growing, you keep cutting, and you keep collecting a paycheck. Since the grass always returns, as long as you perform good work, you don't have to search for a steady stream of new customers. Grass cutters will *never* run out of work. Even in a recession.

But, there is a downside. Grass cutters swap time for money.

- More time *on* the lawn = *more money* in you pocket
- More time *away* from the lawn = *less money* in your pocket

Scenario #2 = the clothes cleaners.

A few friends of mine owned a store called Parkway Cleaners when I was in high school. Well, their dad did. He got into the laundry business when he got out of the army. He made a ton of money washing and ironing everyone's clothes while he was in the military. While others went on leave and took passes, he washed and folded, running his trade there in the barracks (by trading his free time for money).

When he got out of the service, he used the wad of cash to launch the business that he handed off to his two boys. His hard work provided for him, for his kids, for his extended family, for their kids…

(So trading time for money isn't bad– this man clearly left a legacy.)

One day my dad explained to me how clever it was to start something like that cleaning business: "The guy that sells the shirt or pants get paid *one time*," he explained. "He may clear a profit of $2 or $3 by the time his expenses are paid."

Then he hit me with the whammy.

"The guys who *clean* the shirts and pants– like our friends– get paid $2 or $3 *every single time* the shirt gets cleaned. A man will buy a shirt once, but he'll get it laundered dozens of times…"

It's true. And it shows you that selling things that are enjoyed (shirts) is good. Selling services that must be performed again and again (cleaning shirts) is *even better*.

But, as brilliant as it is, it's still a time-for-money exchange.

Scenario #3 = the vending machine business.

My oldest son, Noah, ran a small vending machine business for a few years. He had three machines. I helped him start the business when he was six, taking a few road trips to purchase some machines we found on eBay.

Here's what was great about his vending machines.

1. **The items he sold were *consumable*.** He sold what goes in the machines, the drinks. People bought those all the time. They consumed them, then bought another one. Sometimes they did this multiple times in the same day from the same machine.

2. **The machines worked for him *when he wasn't there*.** When I was cutting grass, I had to show up. No work, no pay. Noah, on the other hand, loaded the machines once a week. He returned a week later to reload them and collect the money he made while he was at home playing with Legos, jumping on his trampoline, and doing his math lessons.

3. **The process was so simple that *almost anyone could do it*.** I don't mean to be disrespectful to my little buddy, but what he did just wasn't that hard of a business model to put together. Anyone else could be trained, including his younger brothers coming

behind him, to do the same thing he did with a virtual guarantee of similar success.

The grass cutting venture, the laundry service, and the vending machines all benefitted from repeat customers. But, the vending machine biz offered a few more benefits which can push you towards financial freedom faster:

- Consumable products
- A process that works even when you're not present
- A simple, duplicable system which almost anyone can do

= DOING SOMETHING WELL, ONE TIME, AND GETTING PAID OVER & OVER & OVER AGAIN...

= HELPS YOU ESCAPE THE "TIME-FOR-MONEY" TRADE

= EMPOWERS YOU TO HAVE BOTH AND

Look at the graphic above. It shows us what happens when we begin leveraging the benefits of residual income. Quite simply, we do something well, one time, and get paid again and again and again… thereby empowering us to escape the time-for-money swap.

I initially thought I would use this book itself as an example of residual income. For sure, it is. I sat down and typed this script, created the graphics, and uploaded the content to the publisher one-time. In turn, I get paid every time the book sells.

However, it's not a duplicatable process. The reality is that in order to "scale this" well beyond my own reach, I'd have to find other authors and content creators. Most people don't create content, though. It's not in there unique skillset. In other words, unlike Noah's vending machine business, writing books isn't duplicatable.

Opportunities that create residual income are the good– the money that shows up again and again. But opportunities which create residual income streams and are repeatable by others are the absolute best– those have exponential potential for growth beyond you. The opportunity with Young Living is similar to Noah's vending business. The vending machines will work on his behalf while he's away, but *he has to continue filling them at regular intervals or the business dries up*.

We feel that multilevel marketing companies provide an incredible opportunity for us to invest in something (a very minimal financial investment at that!) that will continue to grow over time. And **while it does require some continual maintenance, refilling and strategizing, it *doesn't* require a 40 hour workweek to keep moving forward**. Because they are created with a focus on team building, the more support we provide for our team, the more successful our team becomes and in turn the more successful we become. And it's better than filling your "own machines" by yourself.

2. You must to be willing to take an honest look at network marketing

People notoriously equate network marketing (sometimes referred to as "multilevel marketing") with "pyramid schemes."

When asked why they feel like it's a "pyramid scheme," naysayers usually resort to some version of this reply– as if regurgitating a script they've heard somewhere.

"Well, the people at the top make money off of all of the people at the bottom."

Then– "If you don't get in early, you'll never make any money."

I generally tell people that the company with which we're affiliated has been around 25 years. It's still growing. And new members hit the highest ranks every single year. In other words, "getting in early" isn't a valid criticism.

I always ask if they've actually talked to someone who's been successful at network marketing or if they're just sharing what amounts to a quick conclusion that might actually change if they received accurate info. (I've never had anyone who was negative about network marketing admit that they'd spoken with someone who was actually successful in the industry.)

Then, I ask them to take a look at how other organizations are structured. For example, take a look at Walmart's (radically simplified) org chart:

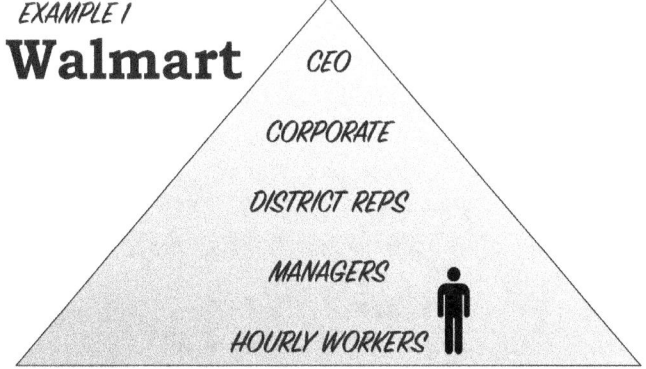

Turns out, Walmart is shaped *exactly* like a pyramid. Now, we expect this from "corporate America." Hence, all the arguments against "the man" and the encouragement to buy local when we can.

Let me show you something strange, though. In fact, let's go religious on this one. The church you attend (or the one you might have grown up attending) is shaped

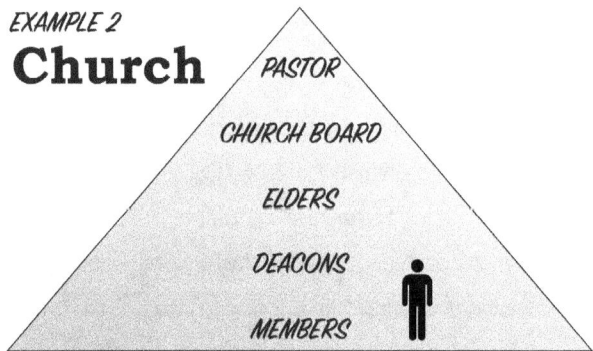

exactly like a pyramid, too.

Notice how the U.S. government functions— just like a pyramid.

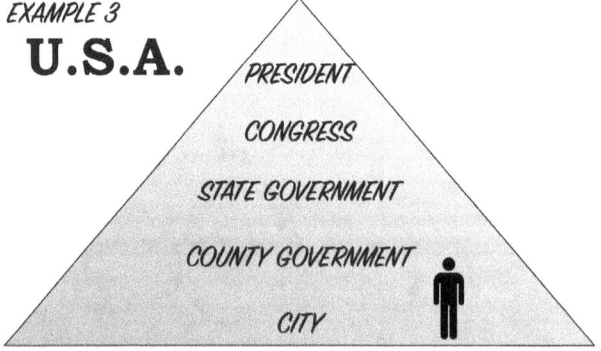

In fact, the organizational structure of your current job is most likely shaped in the same way— with a lot of people on the bottom and progressively fewer and fewer people at the top.

(In each of these pyramids, the higher you rise the more money you make and the greater benefits you receive— because of the people under you.)

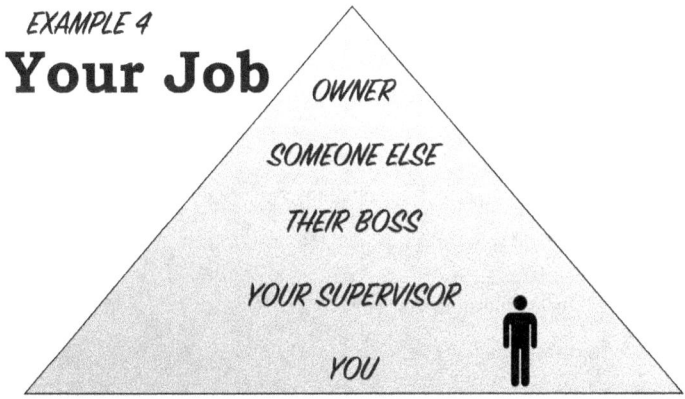

Most retail stores, most churches, most governments, and most employers have internal structures that, when drawn on paper, create a triangle. In other words, **pyramid-shaped organizations are common.**

When people say "pyramid," they usually mean that there's something meant to mislead or defraud people. It's strange, because— again— we're extremely familiar with organizations that have "some people on top." I've often heard the word *scheme* attached to "pyramid"– as in, "you're involved in one of those pyramid schemes."

So, let's define the word *scheme* and see if if fits network marketing. The word *scheme* can be used a noun or a verb. It can be a *thing* (noun) or an *action* (verb).

- *Noun* = a large, systematic plan or arrangement for attaining a particular goal
- *Verb* = devious, with intent to do something illegal or morally wrong

Notice that the noun version of *scheme* is morally "neutral." It's a plan– a method that usually includes steps and processes– to achieve something. In other words, architectural plans are really *schemes* for a house, recipes are *schemes* for cakes and cookies, and budgets are *schemes* to manage your finances.

Far from being the verb form of the word (a moral wrong, with a plan to hurt others), network marketing is radically different than other "pyramid structures" in that network marketing is the only business model (of which I'm aware) in which:

1. The people above you work *for* you (they only succeed by helping you succeed)
2. You can surpass their rank and exceed their income

You may need to read those two points again, because they're the *exact opposite* manner in which most things in our world work.

I wasn't sure about the first point until a guy in my upline saw me working on a project to help him with an event one day. He pulled me to the side…

"I'm thankful you're helping me, but make sure you're not neglecting others who are in your downline by spending time on this with me. I work for you– and you work for them." Then, he added– "If you're working for your upline, you're doing it backwards."

Now, think about his statement compared to the typical business model. In most scenarios the commands flow *down* and the benefits roll *up*. In network marketing, training may flow down, but **benefits only roll up as the people beneath succeed** (I'll come back to this in my epiphany moment in the next chapter in point #5– it was an incredible "ah-hah" moment for me when I truly saw this!).

= A LEGIT BUSINESS MODEL IN WHICH YOU ONLY GROW IF YOU HELP THE PEOPLE "BENEATH YOU" GROW.

= THEY CAN SURPASS YOU + YOU CAN SURPASS OTHERS

Look at the second point above: you can surpass people above you, even exceeding their income. Most of us have been passed over for a promotion. There are only a few positions at the top of any typical organization. And, let's be honest, sometimes, advancement is based more on "who you know" than "what you know" or "what you can do." Somehow, we wrongly import truths about typical organizations into the network marketing world.

I'll tell you my story– and how I fell into the world of network marketing– in chapter 4. Ernie will tell you his in chapter 5. One thing we both had in common was that we didn't want to be like "those people" who are always begging people to buy stuff, and we wanted the business model to work with integrity– not "schemey," in other words.

Here's what I discovered (and what I think you'll see): **the greatest irony of the entire argument is that the "pyramid" that has the greatest chance of empowering your freedom is the one people wrongly accuse of being a scheme**. Do a quick Google search you'll see that network marketing is endorsed by Robert Kiyosaki, Tony Robbins, and Dave Ramsey. And, as each of these well-known leaders suggest, if you follow the masses you will get the same results they've gotten.

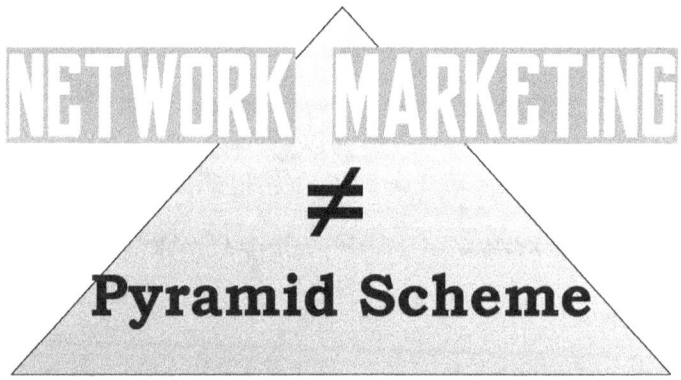

IRONY #1

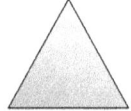
YOU WILL ALWAYS BE LIMITED UNLESS YOU- ODDLY ENOUGH- GET INTO THE ONE PYRAMID PEOPLE ACCUSE OF BEING A "SCHEME."

IRONY #2

IF YOU FOLLOW THE MASSES, YOU WILL GET THE EXACT SAME RESULT THEY'VE GOTTEN!

3. You must be willing to *not* sell a bunch of stuff...

I'm not going to spend a great deal of time on point #3, because we'll dive deep into this one in chapter 8, ("Secret #3 = You Can Do It Without Selling Stuff..."). For now, take a look at the graphic which follows– because it counters another misperception and common caricature of network marketing.

YOU DON'T HAVE TO SELL THINGS...

* *PEOPLE DON'T WANT*
* *PEOPLE DON'T KNOW HOW TO USE*
* *PEOPLE CAN'T AFFORD*
* *PEOPLE BUY ONCE AND THEN ARE DONE*

SEE SECRET #3

People are (wrongly) afraid that if the "sign up" with a network marketing company that they'll have to sell a bunch of stuff that–

- People don't want (you've got to push them to get the sell)

- People don't know how to use (it's not something they would typically be being anyway, thereby making it even more difficult to convince them to make a purchase)

- People can't afford (it has a high price point, requiring lots of convincing)

- People buy once and are done (so you must continue finding new customers in order to keep the income stream coming, meaning most new biz builders income stream evaporates once they run through their friends and family)

What if I told you– and could show you– that none of those things are true?

That would change everything wouldn't it?

Before we move to the final point of this chapter, let's review. So far, I've shown you that in order for this opportunity to work for you, that…

1. You must be open to earning residual income using a duplicatable model

2. You must to be willing to take an honest look at network marketing as a viable business model

3. You must be willing to *not* sell a bunch of stuff

That said, let me show you how the emerging economy actually empowers the opportunity before you.

4. You must take note of the global economic trends— and work with them rather than against them

Think about what would happen if we could look into the future and see how things will unfold. Well, turns out, we can.

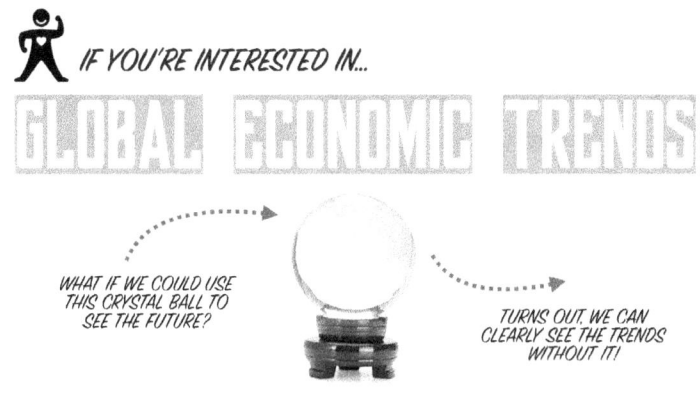

Currently, two trends are emerging with great force. You'll recognize each of them once I mention them. In other words, this doesn't require a crystal ball; it simply requires intentional observation. Here's what's unfolding:

1. **Direct delivery to the consumer** = less emphasis on shopping malls, retail stores, etc.

2. **No inventory or a big investment required to run a business** = easy to go to market.

Let's look at each of those statements.

When I was a child, I loved walking the aisle of Toys 'R Us on Friday evenings with my parents. That was the night we always went out to eat as a family. About 50% of the time my brother and I were able to convince Mom and Dad to take us to look at bikes, skateboards, and video games.

Fast forward 30-plus years…

My youngest boy, Salter, has no idea what Toys 'R Us is. In fact, he doesn't even realize that toy stores were once a thing that you could visit. He only knows of online shopping and book stores (like Barnes & Noble) which now carry as many toys, gifts, and gadgets as they do books.

When he wants a toy, he asks for my smartphone and clicks to the Amazon app. Then, rather than lugging him around town to locate and purchase his newly found treasure, we have it sent directly to the house.

I used to take my four oldest kids to Blockbuster video. The youngest of those four, Levi, always carried a stack of quarters with him, because the nearby Blockbuster would give you a free rental if you got a blue gum ball from their machine (he was content to toss $2.00 of quarters in the machine in order to win a $.99 rental!).

As I was writing this manuscript, I asked him, "Hey, do you remember Blockbuster?"

"No, what's that?" he asked.

"It's the place you took the quarters to win the movies."

"I remember the quarters and the blue gum, but I don't remember the store."

Now, in fairness to him, he was only four when I took him. And that was almost a decade ago. And, since that time, all of the Blockbusters have closed— so there's no evidence sitting around the city to jog his memory. If he wants to watch a movie (which we do a lot!), he sets a time with me to stream it on Netflix, rent it off iTunes, or watch it via Amazon Prime. The youngest kids have *never* been to a Blockbuster or any other video rental store.

You've likely seen the same shifts I have.

Why have these things changed?

Well, **with technological innovation there's been a shift towards direct delivery to the consumer**, thereby removing the middle man from the equation.

Let's look at the second shift– that there's often no inventory or a big investment required.

What would you say if I told you the largest taxi service in the world owns no vehicles, the largest global hotel chain owns no beds and no property, and the largest retailer on the planet owns neither a store nor any inventory?

You might say I'm crazy, yet each of those statements happen to be true. Take a look at this graphic– and even do some fact-checking with these names.

Again, these are the two emerging trends– and they don't seem to be going away. In fact, these trends will likely become more and more firm.

GLOBAL ECONOMIC TRENDS

TREND #1
DIRECT TO THE CONSUMER. LESS EMPHASIS ON SHOPPING MALLS, RETAIL STORES, ETC.

TREND #2
NO INVENTORY OR A BIG INVESTMENT REQUIRED

How does this affect you?

Well, if you can identify an opportunity that empowers your customer base to buy the products on their own (trend #1) and have them shipped to them on demand rather than you having to maintain inventory (trend #2), you've got a potential jetpack.

Should you continue reading?

At the beginning of this chapter I stated that there are four mental shifts you must make in order to make the transition work for you.

1. You must be open to earning residual income using a duplicatable model

2. You must to be willing to take an honest look at network marketing as a viable business model

3. You must be willing to *not* sell a bunch of stuff...

4. You must take note of the global economic trends– and be willing to work with them rather than against them

When we combine each of these together, the results are synergistic. That is, the combined momentum of all four far exceeds the mere sum of the four parts.

1. **Residual Income interests you**
2. **Network Marketing = People above you help you**
3. **You don't want to "sell" stuff**
4. **"Crystal Ball"- New economic trends interest you**

Think back to the villain I mentioned in chapter 2, that time-for-money swap. If you still desire to escape the 9-5, to live well, to do the most good, and to bring others on the journey with you (as you live + work from anywhere) these four trends will be your friends. They are boosters, the multipliers which will add fuel to your jetpack.

In this next chapter I'll share my story– and I'll provide you with some insights I gleaned along the way.

Continue envisioning your own future as you read my story. We're going to provide you the vehicle to get there.

3. MINDSET SHIFT

4. Breaking Through the Glass Ceiling (Finally)

Earlier in the book I mentioned that you may feel like something is holding you back. I suggested the *best* way to break through that "thing," whatever it is, and stop trading time for money, is through network marketing.

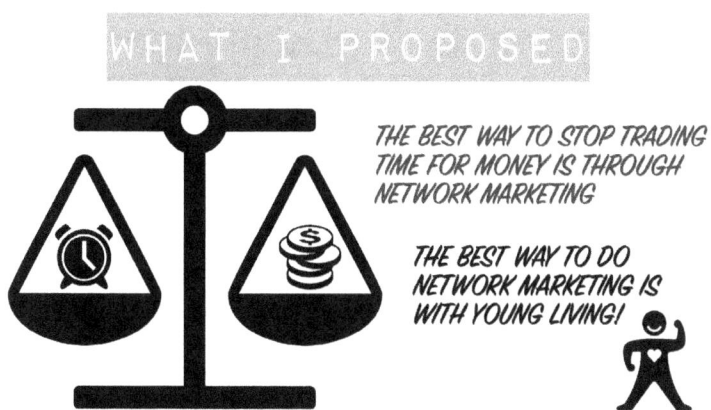

WHAT I PROPOSED

THE BEST WAY TO STOP TRADING TIME FOR MONEY IS THROUGH NETWORK MARKETING

THE BEST WAY TO DO NETWORK MARKETING IS WITH YOUNG LIVING!

We discussed the reasons for that shift in chapter 3. I also mentioned– though I haven't fleshed it out too much– that I believe the best way to do network marketing (not the only way, but the best way) is with Young Living Essential Oils (chapter 2).

I haven't yet relayed my personal experience, though. The truth is that my entry point into this business was a little odd. Here's how it happened…

Eight weeks after she birthed my youngest son, Salter, my (then) wife was invited to a meeting where Young Living essential oils were discussed and taught. Needing a well deserved break out of the house, she loaded the baby and off she went– *just to get out of the house*. She returned a Young Living believer!

Now, she didn't buy anything that night. We had a $100 spending limit, whereby neither of us would ever purchase anything that cost more than that without first having a convo. We didn't have the margin.

So, she returned home and asked about something Young Living called their "Premium Starter Kit." It looked like this–

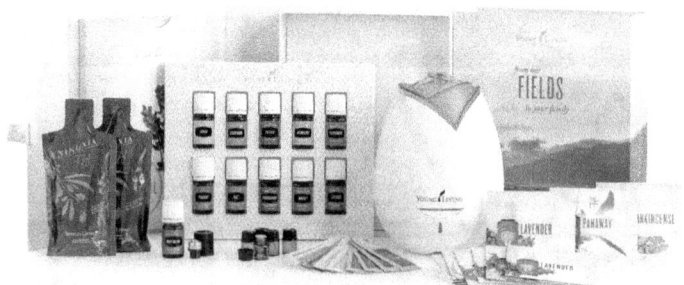

She regularly purchased essential oils, herbs, and other natural remedies from Whole Foods, the farmer's market, and other places, so she used "budget dollars" for this purchase. That is, we didn't have to find "new money" to buy these items. She just swapped money she would have already spent elsewhere and funneled it here.

She honestly never planned to do the business. *Ever.*

However, we traveled to the beach that summer– the week after she received the kit in the mail– and she began using the oils for a few things. She was so surprised with the results that she posted a few pics on Facebook. Others saw those testimonials online and wanted to try the products for themselves. With that, a little biz was "accidentally" born– from a cell phone right there at Orange Beach.

When we returned from vacation, she began holding meetings and teaching about the products, something she never planned to do. Though she originally became a wholesale member of the company just to purchase the products– and nothing more– she saw a viable business opportunity before her.

(That last point is important. Like I mentioned in the previous chapter, you need an opportunity that doesn't require you to "chase people for sales." You need a recession-proof possibility whereby people repeatedly purchase things they already buy every single week, anyway. When this happens, they'll gladly come to you wanting more.)

With the added work load, our 70-80 hour workweek schedule got even tighter. But, and this is key, **the small investment of time + energy we made on the front end returned to us many times over**.

In this chapter, I'm going to tell you my story. Hopefully, this will demonstrate way you need to pay close attention to the remaining pages in the book. You see, I was originally skeptical about the possibilities and what this opportunity could do for us– so much so that I didn't initially do much with the business opportunity.

I'll hit the highlights in five acts:

1. The trip where the "blinders" came off
2. The pivot = "this is real"
3. Lessons learned after going "all in"
4. The shelter was in place for the storm that came
5. My "ah-ha" moment = the biggest success comes from helping others succeed

1. The trip where the "blinders" came off

That beach trip where all the texting and posting about oils took place happened during a hot August. That same month, Young Living announced their first-ever *Drive to Win* contest. Up for grabs was an all-expenses paid trip to a five-star resort in Hawaii. Distributors received points for things like enrolling new members, setting people up on Essential Rewards (and incredible frequent buyer program Young Living has), and helping the members under them also enroll other members.

We heard about the contest after someone in our upline messaged us on our way back from the beach: "Look at the contest leader board– you're on it!"

In part, that was the boost needed to take the business opportunity seriously when we returned from that beach trip.

We were living paycheck-to-paycheck. It seems that during that season, every night as we drifted to bed, we were always deciding whether we should buy one of the kids something they needed or keep the cars running, whether we should pull the money out of savings that we just put in or hold tight until the next payday.

"WE'RE NOT GETTING AHEAD..."

"_____ NEEDS SHOES. I'LL TRANSFER THE $$$ BACK OUT OF SAVINGS WE JUST PUT IN..."

"THE OIL NEEDS TO BE CHANGED. CAN THE POWER BILL WAIT ANOTHER WEEK...?"

"WHERE DID THE WEEK GO? HOW IS IT THURSDAY ALREADY?"

And we were tired. It's hard *not* to feel tired when you're stressed about money.

You might have been there before. You might be there right now.

We were also in one of those seasons when kids' activities were kicking up, when school was beginning to grind, and when added work responsibilities constantly required more and more. It seemed like we were perpetually in one of those seasons eluded to earlier in the book– those times in which your days seem incredibly long, but then you look at the calendar and it's already Thursday. You wonder where the week went, almost as if the time that seemed to move so slowly in the moment suddenly evaporated.

You tell yourself things will get better, but then they don't. They just keep going.

"It's just a season," you say– but unlike the weather the season never changes.

We didn't have margin– neither the time or the money– for a vacation like the award trip. But, when we finished in the Top 10 in a global contest, we were invited to attend. We won 8th place in the world. And that changed everything.

Now, before I go farther, I want to remind you…

We were dancing the time-for-money tango. We just weren't doing a very good job of it. Furthermore– and **this is important to remember– we were "doing everything right."**

This is important. In chapter 1 I mentioned 5 issues that we sometimes confront. Notice the last two.

- Point #4– You might feel like the current system is set up to enslave – not empower

- Point #5– You might feel like you're being held back instead of being helped up

These two seemed to weigh on me. No, I wasn't playing the victim– and don't do so now. However, I am honest about where things stand.

THINGS THAT WERE TRUE OF ME

* I GRADUATED FROM COLLEGE + GRADUATE SCHOOL
* I WASN'T LAZY- DURING SOME SEASONS I WORKED 2 JOBS!
* I WAS "DOING EVERYTHING RIGHT"
* I WANTED TO SPEND MORE TIME WITH MY FAMILY, BUT COULDN'T
* I LIKED MY JOB, BUT I FELT STUCK IN IT
* I LEFT GRAD SCHOOL WITH $35,000 IN STUDENT LOAN DEBT
* I WAS WORKING IN AN AREA RELATED TO MY EDUCATION

The truth is that **we didn't have enough time or money, yet I had done exactly what I had been trained (by society) to do from a young age**:

- I graduated from college and graduate school (I have seven years of post-high school education)

- I wasn't lazy– there was rarely a season in which I didn't work at least two jobs

- I was doing "everything right"

- I wanted to spend more time with my family, but couldn't (i.e., I didn't have any hobbies outside of the house– didn't have time for them)

- I liked my job, but I felt stuck in it– I would never be able to financially get ahead if I continued along that career path
- I left graduate school with $35,000 in student loan debt
- I was working in an area related to my education (so I couldn't blame this on something like "if I could just get into my field of expertise…")

The picture on the previous page summarizes my dilemma perfectly.

2. The pivot = "this is real"

The Hawaii trip accomplished two things for me:

1. I saw the importance of regaining my health
2. I saw the business opportunity before me

First, I saw the importance of regaining my health. With the time-for-money suck that had been happening for the previous decade, I'd let my health go. Whereas I'd once been athletically trim, I was now… well… festively plump.

While on that trip, I saw myself full length in a mirror. We didn't have a full length mirror in our home, so this was the first true gaze I'd gotten in a long time.

Even though I would occasionally bump into friends from high school and notice that *they* looked a bit older and significantly more robust, somehow I'd mentally excluded myself from those changes. In my mind, I still looked the same, never aging, immune to the gravity of time and inactivity, un-phased by the caloric intake of sugary sodas. Never mind the fact I'd been dodging the scale, didn't like seeing pics of myself, and kept eating like a human vacuum cleaner.

While on that trip I decided to reclaim my health. I returned home and began eating right and exercising immediately. With the help of some of the products in Young Living's arsenal (protein shakes, oils for recovery, etc.), I began shed about 2.5 pounds per week! I eventually lost 50 and am now in better shape than I've ever been.

Second, I saw (firsthand) that network marketing is a viable business opportunity. Although I didn't initially believe it, I *quickly* saw the truth.

On the final leg of our flight on the way there, I found myself in a convo. It was somewhere over the Pacific, about 300 miles from LAX.

"Some people make $30,000 a month doing this," someone told me.

After a few moments, I sought clarification: "They earn that by selling essential oils and personal care products and supplements and...?"

"They don't really *sell* them, but yeah. They make that kind of money. I know some of them."

"You, yourself?" I clarified. "You *personally* know someone who makes that?"

That first evening in Hawaii I met a handful of people I knew only from online interaction via Facebook and email. I cornered them (politely) and asked them if this was a legitimate opportunity or if we had just gotten lucky and won a trip.

"It's real," one guy– who became a close friend– said.

"How real? Are *you* actually making money from this?"

He was. The previous month's check was $27,000. The current month's was $35,000. These weren't random checks posted to the Internet– these were numbers from people I actually knew and trusted.

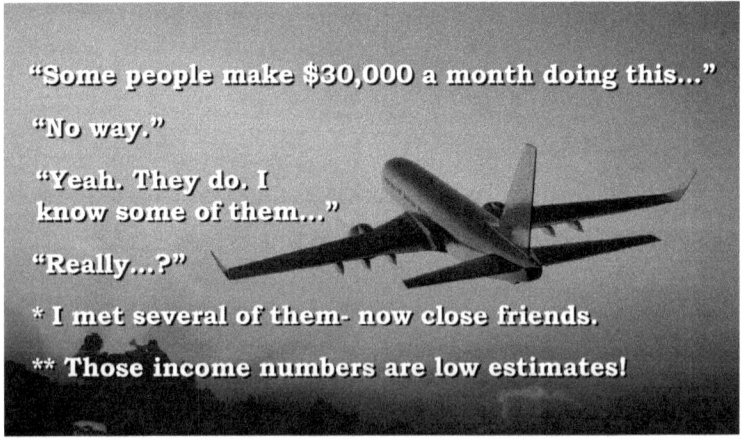

"Some people make $30,000 a month doing this..."
"No way."
"Yeah. They do. I know some of them..."
"Really...?"
* I met several of them- now close friends.
** Those income numbers are low estimates!

In addition, I met the founders of Young Living, as well as some of the executive staff. We received an "up close and personal" look at the farms where the products came from. I was ready to charge full speed ahead.

3. Lessons learned after going "all in"

At the same time we took the trip to Hawaii, a nonprofit I led was in the middle of a massive project. Specifically, we were opening a thrift store. Since we were in the early stages of launching that Young Living business at the exact same time, I had a front row seat to watch both opportunities unfold concurrently.

One day I sat down and compared, side-by-side, what it looked like to strenuously start that thrift store compared to launching our network marketing business. I identified at least 8 differences– all of which were in favor of the home business.

The variances ranged from everything related to start-up capital that was required to managing payroll, facilities, and employees to the learning curve and the financial exposure you have if you fail. This was such a pervasive lesson for me that I dedicated an entire chapter to this comparison in *The Guys' Guide to Oils*. You can download chapter 16, "Bankrupt from a Thrift Store," free of charge or watch the video comparison at OilyApp.com/ThriftStore.

THE THRIFT STORE VS. YOUNG LIVING

	THRIFT STORE	HOME BIZ
1. START-UP CAPITAL REQUIRED	$60,000 AND GROWING- EVEN WITH ALL THE DEALS WE GOT	< $200
2. INVENTORY + INVENTORY MANAGEMENT	YES	No inventory required. Can manage as much / little as you want
3. PAYROLL- MANAGE IT?	YES	No
4. BUILDINGS & UTILITIES	YES	Run it from our house, utilities paid for when we pay our normal monthly expenses
5. ADVERTISING	SOME	As much / little as you want
6. HOURS REQUIRED / WEEK	STAFF COVERING 80-PLUS HOURS / WEEK	You decide
7. LEARNING CURVE	STEEP AND COMES FAST	Learn as you go, at your own pace
8. FINANCIAL EXPOSURE IF YOU FAIL	YES- MAJOR LOSS- AND YOU LOSE MONEY AND TIME THAT COULD HAVE BEEN INVESTED SOMEWHERE ELSE	None- you spent <$200 on products you would have likely bought anyway

Here's something else I learned when I went "all in." Though my exposure and my effort were increasing with every new project we undertook in the typical business model, my paycheck remained flat. In fact, here's a look at it over a 21-month period. That flat line represents about $6,000 per month, including insurance and all other benefits (and we had 11 people living in our house at that time).

MY FULL-TIME PAYCHECK

Now, let me show you something.

When you set the network marketing paycheck beside my full-time paycheck, you notice a few things:

- **The network marketing check starts small— so it seems relatively insignificant in the beginning.** In fact, a lot of people I know who tried network marketing quit, after deciding that they're not getting paid what they're worth.

- **The check grows.** As you continue earning while you learn and learning while you earn, your skill level increases. And, at some point, you break through the time-for-money barrier. (We talk discuss earning while you learn in chapter 7.)

Here's a look at both checks over that same 21-month period. I've highlighted the beach trip where the business began, the trip to Hawaii where the blinders came off, and the moment I decided I could work from home full time.

COMPARISON

Bar chart showing growth with markers at BEACH TRIP ($0.00), HAWAII (~$7,500.00), and WORK FROM HOME (~$15,000.00), with final bar reaching $22,500.00.

During the first month we made about $150. We recovered almost *all* our initial "investment." Plus, we received products in exchange for that money– items we would have purchased that month anyway. And, the prices weren't inflated– we received over $360 for the less-than-$200 we spent.

(Remember, those were "budget dollars." We would have purchased those items *somewhere* that month if we hadn't bought them from Young Living.)

If we walked away from the opportunity at that point, this would have been a great deal. But look what happened…

VITAL STATS

MONTH 1 MADE ABOUT $150
MONTH 4 RIVALED A FULL-TIME TEACHER'S SALARY
MONTH 7 MADE AN AVERAGE "FULL TIME" INCOME
MONTH 12 EARNED 5 FIGURES PER MONTH FOR FIRST TIME
MONTH 18 BROKE $20K / MONTH FOR FIRST TIME
MONTH 22 I QUIT MY FULL TIME JOB

Now, let me be transparent. We worked. A lot. So this wasn't free money. But, it facilitated freedom. And that's what we're looking for.

4. The shelter was in place for the storm that came

About three years into the business venture, we took a trip to California. My wife attended a workshop for a few weeks and I managed the kids and worked from home at an AirBNB rental.

In the middle of that conference, I had a work trip of my own– a retreat. That's a pic of me below, after walking on fire at the conclusion of the workshop. The network marketing / work-from-home opportunity had provided me with just that– a chance to walk on fire. Little did I know just "real life" that metaphor would be, though.

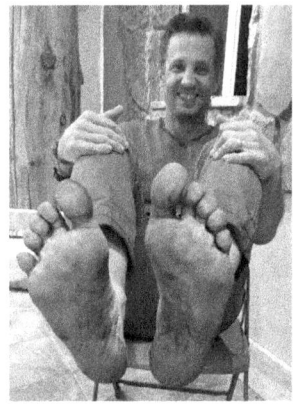

The final night of the retreat I received a call "from home" (i.e., the AirBNB). One of our biological kids revealed that one of our adopted boys had been inappropriate with him. In fact, he had done so with two of the bios and the other adopted boy.

Life took a rather quick turn. Things became topsy-turvy fast. I thought we had been finding our groove. Little did I know I had been living the "calm before the storm."

The next several months– even year– were filled with endless meetings, counseling appointments, group home visits, and even legal proceedings. It's amazing how fast life can flip.

At some point I actually said, "**I don't know how someone would be able to manage this– and show up for all of this– if they had a full-time job to maintain**."

I didn't have a full time job, though. I was blessed with a greater degree of freedom than I'd ever experienced. I didn't have to exchange time for money. I could keep that time, use it for the family issues that needed to be addressed, and still have some money for the bills and the groceries and our other needs.

CRISIS IN OUR HOME
REQUIRED TOTAL TIME + ATTENTION

WORKED FAR LESS
STILL GOT PAID

That's when it hit me: **Stepping away from the time-for-money tango isn't *only* about freedom to do the things you *want* to do.** Notice, I haven't mentioned dream vacations, fancy houses, or fast cars at all in this book. I never used the money for any of those things. **True freedom is the capacity to do the things you *need* to do.**

GETTING OFF THIS TRADE ISN'T JUST ABOUT THE FREEDOM TO DO THE THINGS YOU WANT TO DO...

IT'S FREEDOM TO DO THE THINGS YOU NEED TO DO!

You might have grown up with the mindset that "money is evil." Some people erroneously suggest the Bible teaches as much. It doesn't. Rather, it cautions us that the *love* of money is the root cause of much of the evil we see (1 Timothy 6:10).

Money, in and of itself (like the word *scheme*), is neutral– *neither good or bad*.

In other words, dollars are like bricks. You can use bricks to build a house or you can use them to break windows. You can use them to create a shelter or you can use them to destroy.

Money is the same way. It can be used for noble or dishonorable purposes alike. And the more you have, the more graciously grand or radically evil you can do. It works both ways.

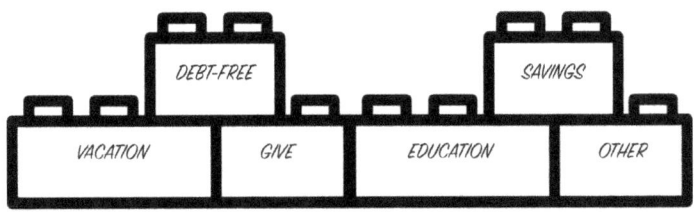

(I saw this firsthand when one of the distributors with Young Living travelled to Ecuador to visit the school our company helped build. He mentioned that the bus they had been using broke down and kids were now walking 3-4 hours to school every day. He suggested we rally the men in our online group together and purchase a new one. In less than a month, the men raised $145,000 to handle this need.)

So far, I've led you through the first 4 acts of my entry into network marketing.

1. The Hawaii trip where the "blinders" came off
2. The pivot = this is real (the actions I took post-Hawaii)
3. Lessons learned after going "all in" (and my thrift store comparison)
4. The shelter was in place for the storm that came

Let me preference the fifth and final act with a question…

Do you remember in the previous chapter (during point #2, where I introduced network marketing) when I talked about your upline actually working for you instead of you working for them?

I didn't understand the full *gravitas* of that concept until we reached one of the first leadership ranks . Let me explain…

5. My "ah-ha" moment = the biggest success comes from helping others succeed

One of the first things I did when I got involved in network marketing is read the compensation plan. Now, that's not something I advise everyone to spend time doing– you can succeed without understanding all the intricacies and nuances. I read it because I was skeptical that you could actually make money in this business (unless you were the first in), and– if you could make money– I wanted to see exactly what you needed to do in order to get paid.

Here's what I discovered:

- **Companies pay a relatively low percentage on goods that are purchased through your downline (i.e., your organization)**. Of course, when you add "a bunch of a little" together, the numbers can be staggering. But, since you're *not* paid off of everyone in your downline (that's another misperception– the people "at the top" don't make money off everyone), the number remains relatively low.

- **Companies pay the biggest bonuses to you when you help others in your organization reach significant milestones as business builders**. Remember, your upline works for you!

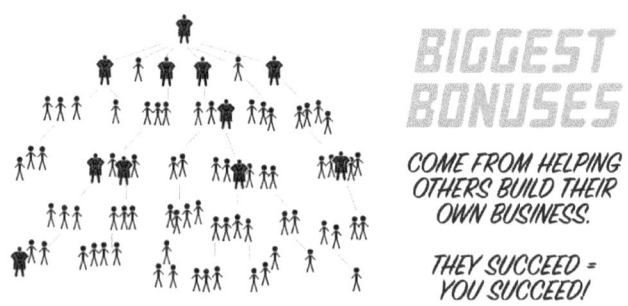

After reading the compensation plan, I decided to do some fact checking from the field. I reached out to some trusted friends.

I opened a group chat and asked them via Facebook Messenger: "Send me a breakdown of your check– just the percentages. What's the percentage you have for commissions off purchases in your organization as compared to the two different types of bonuses you receive for empowering new leaders?"

Here's what I found out (though I won't share their numbers with you, some of them did just send me the raw data and said, "Go figure it out…"):

- **All of these guys are doing extremely well.** If you keep working the business with intentionality, you can make a lot of money.

- Oddly enough, **they all have radically different sized organizations**, with volume ranking anywhere from annual sales in the ten millions down to volume around $400,000 per year.

- **All of the guys are making about the same amount of commission via the percentage off sales**, regardless of how large the organization is (again, contrary to popular belief, you *do not* "get paid" off everyone in your downline.)

- The biggest factor in paycheck size, then, was not the overall volume of their organization. At some point, unless you keep building "wide," that percentage *seems* to max out. **The biggest factor was how many leaders they had beneath them.** In other words, **the key factor in a large paycheck, in this unscientific experiment, turned out to be** *helping others find time + money freedom.*

This was my "ah-ha" moment. Yes, we were successful when we began receiving larger and larger paychecks. And we celebrated achievements like matching the full-time income I was earning– and then even doubling it. But, **we were the most successful– and our checks grew even larger– the more we empowered others to take that journey for themselves**.

In fact, I made it my goal at that point to identify 50 people and help them reach a full-time by working from anywhere– even if they kept their day job.

That's my story and I'm sticking to it

So that's part of my story– the part about network marketing, anyway. And it's how I began shifting…

- From 60-80 hour work weeks outside of the home to working from home (or anywhere else)

- From tanking my health because I was juggling so many balls I didn't have time to take care of myself to learning to steward my physical and emotional wellbeing

- From missing the kids and significant moments in their lives to enjoying life with them

- From arriving late for dinner 3-4x per week to enjoying any meals I want to share with my family, regardless of the time of day it is

- From struggling paycheck-to-paycheck to having enough to share with others

But this isn't just my story. In the next chapter, you'll hear from my friend Ernie. And, as you read, remember this could be your story, too.

5. "Normal" People Doing Real Life

NOTE: CHAPTER 5 IS WRITTEN BY ERNIE YARBROUGH. ERNIE IS ONE OF THE FOUNDERS OF OILYAPP. HE AND HIS WIFE, MYRA, ARE NOT ONLY IN MY UPLINE; THEY'VE REACHED THE HIGHEST RANK IN THE COMPANY.

So far in our lives, it seems that the paths we have taken and the decisions we have made that have impacted us the most have not been the "big ones." As one man noted, it's usually those small and seemingly insignificant decisions that end up having the most amazing and life-changing results.

As I write this, I sit on a plane returning home from Tanzania where I was privileged to climb Mt. Kilimanjaro with 21 other people as we sought to bring awareness and resources to the fight against modern human trafficking. And this adventure of a lifetime all started from the same "insignificant" decision that lead my wife Myra and me into the use of essential oils.

The picture above follows is my brother-in-law, Jacob (left), along with Andy (center) and me on our way to the summit.

Myra had worked for several years in the field of her college degree (interior design) at a high-end furniture store until I was able to graduate with an electrical engineering degree and move into full time work in the steel industry. When I graduated, she was 7 months pregnant and expecting our first child, so she came home to be a full-time mother.

When the economy crashed in 2008, I was working swing shift for a local steel mill and had to pick up a second job on my off days just to cover the mortgage. For about a year I barely saw my wife and newborn son as I travelled multiple states servicing emergency lighting for different stores. We had a mortgage *and* we had racked up credit card debt.

Stay at home mom finds a hobby

With me gone so much, she turned her love for beauty and family into a blog so she could share her passion– how to make your home and family as beautiful as possible. She worked 80-90 hours per week, teaching herself how to create content, how to maneuver basic HTML, CSS and JavaScript, how to productively use social media, and how to authentically engage an audience with her heart for beauty. It wasn't very long before her blog traffic began to really pick up and she was introduced into the world of ad networks and blog monetization.

Somewhere along the way, my wife had a "random" and "insignificant" meeting on Twitter with a lady named Alyssa. Almost immediately a friendship was formed. They shared a love for blogging, attended blogging conferences together, and developed a friendship which continues to this day.

Alyssa introduced us to essential oils. After eventually stepping back from the blog world, she flew out to visit us all the way from Texas. She spent time with Myra and our small family. Before leaving, she pulled out her "bag of oils" and introduced us to the world of Young Living.

Myra and I had both grown up with naturally minded parents, so the idea of essential oils made sense. **We never balked at the idea of oils– it was the model of network marketing that gave us serious concerns.**

Our only experiences with direct sales up to that point had been negative– they were far too expensive to join and far too focused on the wrong things. Big houses, fancy cars, expensive vacations, large boats– we had seen all these used as motivation to join, and all of those things turned us off. Those things don't resonate with who we are.

We have to be able to share something because we believe in it. Our passion has to resonate from a place of genuine love, sincerity and belief. We are sharers, not salespeople. We wanted to live from the overflow of abundant grace, not the overflow of materialistic pretense.

We loved and trusted Alyssa, so we cautiously agreed to try the oils with one caveat – we would never "do" the business. We would only try them for their own benefits, on their own merits. We weren't going to "sign people up." We were only going to use the product for our family and see what happened.

So that's what we did.

Alyssa knew this about us, and she knew what Young Living's oils could do. So I guess she kinda set us up. We are forever thankful she did!

An accidental business

After a few weeks on the shelf, Myra decided to open her kit and give it a try. The good results for our family were immediate. And because Myra never keeps a good thing to herself, she started weaving those benefits into her blog because– just like she wanted to share with others how to make delicious meals and how to beautifully decorate their homes in a budget friendly way– she wanted to share with others the benefits she was experienced with essential oils.

That's just who she is. And because her (by now) large reader base had come to know and love her, their interest was immediate.

People wanted to get oils the same way she had. People began purchasing products, and stories and thank you notes began to pour in via email as these same people shared with Myra the benefits they were seeing for their families.

I distinctly remember (more than once!) coming home from my engineering job to see her sitting on the sofa crying unexpected tears of joy as she shared with me these emails. I realized something special was happening. I knew I could support my wife in this endeavor.

But is it real?

I just had one hesitation before I could speak publicly in support of Young Living as a company, a business opportunity, and a source of health products. **I needed to make sure that their corporate culture matched what I was seeing take place in my wife**.

With this in mind, my wife took me to my first event in Birmingham, Alabama. By this point *she* knew what the corporate culture was, but she knew my concerns and desires were sincere and she knew that I had to be convinced for myself. We went and spent the next couple of days with around 2,000 moms and dads as we heard all about Young Living's products, its mission, and its purpose.

It was unlike any network marketing meeting I had ever experienced. I had walked into previous meetings only to hear songs about wanting to be rich. I walked into this Young Living event only to hear things like "we make a product for a purpose, not a profit" and "we are so committed to helping others with the finest quality products that we will take a product out of stock and wait for another harvest rather than sale synthetic replacements."

No songs about money. No hype. No rah-rah.

In fact, I heard only one sentence about money over two days, directing people to talk to their upline if they wished to pursue a business.

"If you're interested in learning more, you should talk to them," the speaker said. "The paychecks can be pretty good."

That was it.

The entire focus was on helping people with naturally grown and naturally sustainable products. And how their commitment to quality would never be comprised in their mission to put oils in every home in the world.

I was so excited!

I continued to attend events with my wife, and the belief only became stronger– the authenticity and sincerity of Young Living corporate matched what I saw happening in my wife.

Looking back, living forward

It's hard to believe that "little meeting" with Alyssa was almost 7 years ago. Wow, how the time has flown! What a different path God has taken us on!

By God's blessing, my wife has achieved the highest rank in the company. I've been able to hang up my corporate cleats for other purposes and passions He has called me to. And we've been entrusted with the tremendous privilege and responsibility of caring for over 50,000 people on our team.

We *love* using business as a means of loving, encouraging and ministering to others.

We *love* helping others see and accomplish their goals of freedom and joy in their health, homes and even in their finances.

We *love* that we get to do all of this in a way that aligns with who we are at our very core– thankful recipients of God's marvelous grace.

Content in all circumstances

We know what it is to have little. We know what it is to have a little extra. Either way, **we know that true joy comes not from material possessions but from living in the calling and purpose for which we were created**. This business platform provided the opportunity to do just that.

It is in that joy that we stand, and in that joy that we extend our hands to our team and to you with the hope that we can find together what we were never meant to find on our own– fullness of joy by living on the outside what we are called to be on the inside.

Our team name is Vibrant Essentials. I think that name sums it up quite well.

+++++++++

Maybe your story resonates with Ernie's. I know my does…

Remember my story?

> **REMEMBER MY STORY?**
>
> * I GRADUATED FROM COLLEGE + GRADUATE SCHOOL
> * I WASN'T LAZY- DURING SOME SEASONS I WORKED 2 JOBS!
> * I WAS "DOING EVERYTHING RIGHT"
> * I WANTED TO SPEND MORE TIME WITH MY FAMILY, BUT COULDN'T
> * I LIKED MY JOB, BUT I FELT STUCK IN IT
> * I LEFT GRAD SCHOOL WITH $35,000 IN STUDENT LOAN DEBT
> * I WAS WORKING IN AN AREA RELATED TO MY EDUCATION

Like me, Ernie did all the things right. He went to school. He got a job– and was even willing to work a second one.

And though he wasn't primarily motivated by the money, he knew he needed resources in order to cover his living expenses. In other words, the things that should have guaranteed success didn't.

In Part 2 of the book we'll outline 3 secrets *they* don't want you to know. Those secrets are:

- Secret #1 = You must own + invest to get ahead

- Secret #2 = You can earn while you learn (and learn while you earn)

- Secret #3 = You can do it without selling stuff that people don't want, people don't know how to use, people can't afford, and people buy once and forget about

Let's keep moving. I'll show you how you can achieve each of these three through this process– even if you don't have a lot of time or money to spare.

5. "NORMAL" PEOPLE DOING REAL LIFE

Part 2 = Three Secrets *They* Don't Want You to Know

6. Secret #1 = You Must Own + Invest to Get Ahead

For the past 90-ish pages, I've done my best to demonstrate that in order to truly live a life of freedom you've got to position ourself to stop trading time for money.

Furthermore, I've added that:

1. The *best* (not the only) way to stop trading time for money is through network marketing, *and*
2. The *best* (not the only) way to do network marketing is with Young Living

My assumption is that if I prove those two points to you, then you'll want to begin working with us– and use this a possible piece in your pursuit of living the life your meant to live.

Here's what my goal looks like visually:

MY GOAL = SHOW YOU >>>

THE BEST WAY TO STOP TRADING
TIME FOR MONEY IS THROUGH
NETWORK MARKETING, AND

THE BEST WAY TO DO NETWORK
MARKETING IS WITH YOUNG LIVING!

IF I SHOW YOU THAT THIS IS TRUE,
YOU'LL WANT TO WORK WITH US...

Along the journey towards freedom, you confront a financial reality that many business gurus never tell you the truth. **They rarely explain to you you'll never get ahead unless you own and invest**. That is, without making that leap, you'll find yourself stuck in a holding pattern, forever working for someone else— someone who will gladly exchange some of your time for more money. You'll find yourself forever doomed to dance that tricky time-for-money tango.

"TO BECOME FINANCIALLY
FREE, YOU MUST MOVE
THROUGH THE QUADRANTS
AND GET TO THE BUSINESS
OWNER & INVESTOR STAGES
AS QUICKLY AS POSSIBLE."

Robert Kiyosaki, *Rich Dad, Poor Dad*

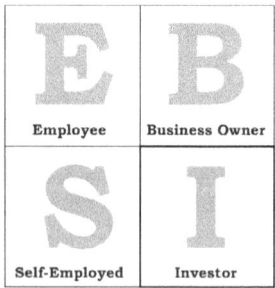

Robert Kiyosaki, the author of *Rich Dad, Poor Dad*, rightfully (and eloquently) argues that in order to become financially free we've got to move through four quadrants– as quickly as possibly– and arrive at the Business Owner and Investor stages.

His four "Cash Flow Quadrants" are:

1. Employee
2. Self-Employed
3. Business Owner
4. Investor

There's a logical progress to the movement.

First, most of us begin as employees– we work for someone else. They give us their money in exchange for our time. This is true of everyone from the minimum-age earner at the coffee shop to the school teacher to the government official to the woman who just graduated law school and took a job downtown.

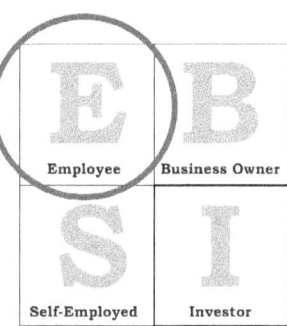

EMPLOYEE = **YOU WORK FOR SOMEONE ELSE (BOTTOM OF THE PYRAMID)**

Second, many of us become self-employed– we do projects whereby we create income streams that provide us with money in exchange for time. This category is tricky, because it's easy to confuse "Business Owner" with this designation.

About a decade ago, I worked at a nonprofit in town. Faith-based, they had a full-time pastor on staff.

"I have a business on the side," he told me.

"Oh, what do you do?" I asked.

I was intrigued. I was in the middle of my 60-80 hour a week mad dash (a sprint I ran for 15+ years), and wanted to know if perhaps there was a way out for me, too.

"I have a fish and chips place," he answered. Then– "It's a little space I rent from the gas station down the street. We open up in the afternoons and on the weekends."

"Who works it?"

"My wife and I."

"You mean that you do *that business* along with the other things you have going on *here* at the ministry center?"

He explained that he did. And he detailed how either he or his wife were always there, how they handed-off car-pool responsibilities to each other, effectively tag-teaming everything they needed to do in order to keep the household, their day jobs, and that business a float.

After hearing him paint the portrait of all the hoop-jumping, long-hours, and over-complicated planning this all entailed, I offered, "Sounds a like *a lot* to me."

"It is," he offered, not missing a beat. "But we've always wanted to own a business, and now we do."

After pondering his answer *silently*, I thought *to myself,* "You don't own a business. That business owns you. **That business is nothing more than a job you've created for yourself, a place where you're effectively the *only* employee**. If you don't show up, you don't get paid. And, even if you don't, you're still responsible for all the bills required to keep that place open…"

Or, to say it another way, "You're just trading time for money in a different format."

SELF-EMPLOYED = YOU
WORK FOR YOURSELF- BUT
THE JOB OWNS YOU!
NO WORK = NO PAY.
YOU ARE THE BUSINESS.

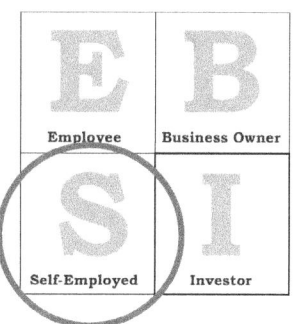

That's the "trick" about the Self-Employed quadrant. As Kiyosaki explains, *you are the business.* **It *seems* like you have a business, but you most often *don't*. The business has you.**

Now, there's nothing wrong with Self-Employment (left bottom). It can offer you a greater degree of freedom than being an Employee (left top). My books and many of the resources I create fall under the guise of the Self-Employment box. But, it's important that we understand the difference between being an Employee (of ourselves, that is, Self-Employed) and being a Business Owner.

The third category, Business Owner (top right), works different than Self-Employment. The main difference is this: a business "works" and you get paid *even when you're not there.*

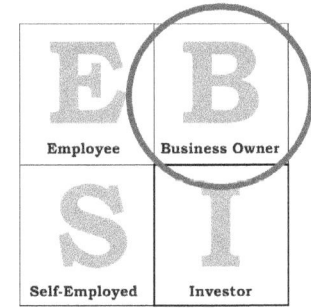

BUSINESS OWNER = **THE BUSINESS "WORKS" AND YOU GET PAID- EVEN WHEN YOU'RE NOT THERE!**

Here are a two questions to ask when considering the difference between Self-Employed (bottom left) and Business Owner (top right):

- *Does the business continue when I'm not there (i.e., can I take a vacation and still get paid)?*

- *Could the entity exist if I walk away permanently (or it it hitched to me being present)?*

If you can't answer "yes" to *both* of the questions above, you don't have a business. You might in the early stages of a business, but you're still self-employed. And that means you're still in the time-for-money tango.

The fourth category, Investor (bottom right) is yet another step in our progression. At this point, you invest in other people's businesses– meaning you get paid for a business you don't even manage.

INVESTOR = YOU USE YOUR MONEY TO INVEST IN OTHER PEOPLE'S BUSINESSES... YOU DON'T EVEN HAVE TO MANAGE THE BUSINESS TO GET PAID.

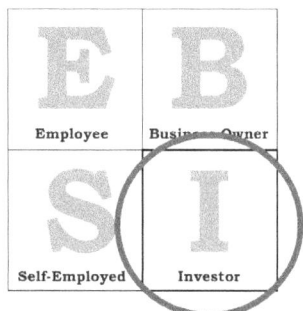

So how do you get there?

If you're living (as I was) paycheck-to-paycheck, you might think, "Yeah, that sounds great… but I don't have a way in. I'll be *forever* stuck at the Employee quadrant."

In other words, you're aware that the cost of starting any business is unattainable for most people.

The truth is that most business *are* out of reach for the vast majority of people. I did a quick Google search and found the following associated with a new start-up:

- Food truck = $28,000–$114,000

- Thrift store = about $100,000 (my experience was that even with donated goods was $80,000 to launch and $60,000 month in expenses to maintain– I wrote about this in point 3 of chapter 4)

- 7/11 Convenient Store = $150,000 in liquid assets, as well as a net worth of $250,000

- Licensed Starbucks = $315,000, plus monthly costs

- Panera Bread = $1.6 million

If you were qualified for *any* of these opportunities, you probably wouldn't be looking for "something else" right now. You'd be in a different place already.

Now, if you had $100,000 to invest right now and you could earn 4% per year (which you probably could *not* do– my money market account earns less than 2%!), you would receive $4,000 per year in return– or about $333 per month. If you had $1,000,000 to invest at the same rate, you could receive (by the same calculations) about $3,330 each month.

Young Living's income disclosure statement (they release this every other year or so, noting the average amounts they paid to distributors of different ranks) reveals something incredible (See YoungLiving.com/IDS for the latest info. These results were published on the 2018 income disclosure statement, accessed April 2, 2020):

- The average Gold-ranking member earned $47,253 ($3,939 per month)

- The average Platinum-ranking member earned $117,949 ($9,929 per month)

- The average Diamond-ranking member earned $313,866 ($26,156 per month)
- The average Royal Crown Diamond-ranking member earned $1,538,528 ($128,211 per month)

Working a Young Living membership as a business (which, consequently, is willable and sellable) provides you the opportunity to accomplish both quadrants on the right side of Kiyosaki's equation. That is, the best way to become both a Business Owner (right top) and Investor (right bottom) is network marketing.

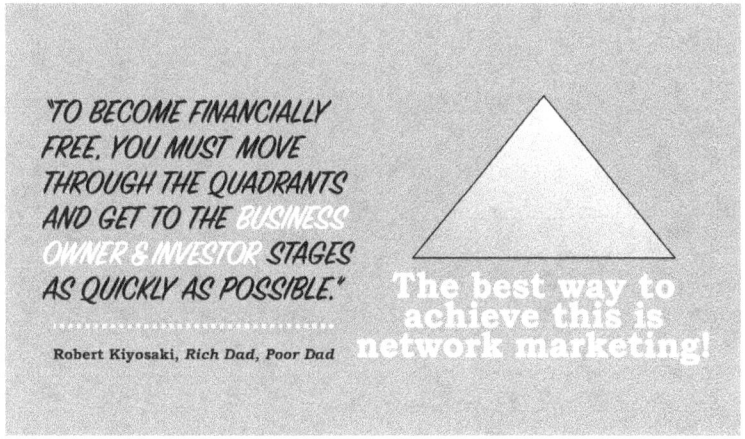

Remember, in chapter 3 (point #2) I showed you that this isn't a pyramid scheme. You don't have to be in "first" in order to achieve success. You simply need to "get in" and begin working the system that's in place, trusting that you'll get similar results to others who work the process.

That invariably leads to a few questions:

- Question 1: *Do I have to sell stuff to all of my friends and family?*

    No. I'll explain why in Secret #3 (chapter 8).

- Question 2: *Do I have to invest a lot of money on the front end in order to buy shelves full or products to stash in my living room or my garage?*

    No. I will outline that in Secret #3 also.

- Question 3: *Will you or the person "above" me get rich off me?*

    Nope– unless I (or they) make you "rich." Go back to the "ah-ha" moment I had (point 3 in chapter 4).

- Question 4: *How can I trust the quality?*

    Well, as the next picture show, it's easy to control the product when you own the farms. Plus, the company has been around for 25 years. There's been ample time for the organization to be thoroughly vetted.

YOU CAN CONTROL THE QUALITY WHEN YOU OWN THE FARMS!

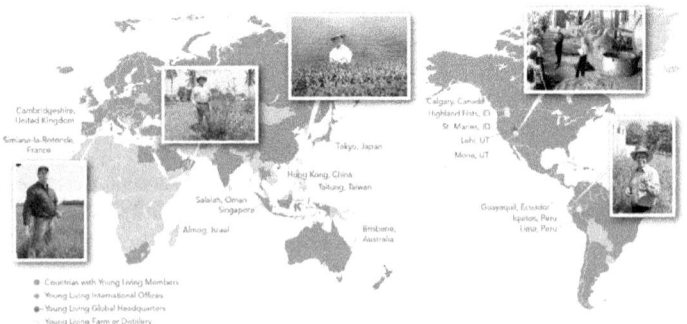

In 2019 I snapped a photo of the company's growth trends. Whereas the normal life cycle of network marketing companies include a few early years of quick growth followed by a short plateau and then a crash, notice that Young Living has been growing steadily for 25 years.

Yes, there's been an uptick in recent years, but not until well after the company had become well established and began opening new markets around the world. And, as the global trends continue taking root (point #4 in chapter 3), natural health products and direct-to-consumer delivery will continue becoming the norms.

Conclusion

At the beginning of the chapter I told you that Secret #1 is that you must own + invest to get ahead. You can't shoot for mere employment or even self-employment. You must move to the right side of Robert Kiyosaki's four quadrants.

- You become a Business Owner by launching your own organization.

- You become an Investor by leading others who want to escape the tyranny of the time-for-money tango to do the same thing. As you help them succeed you are financially rewarded for funneling time and effort into helping them grow.

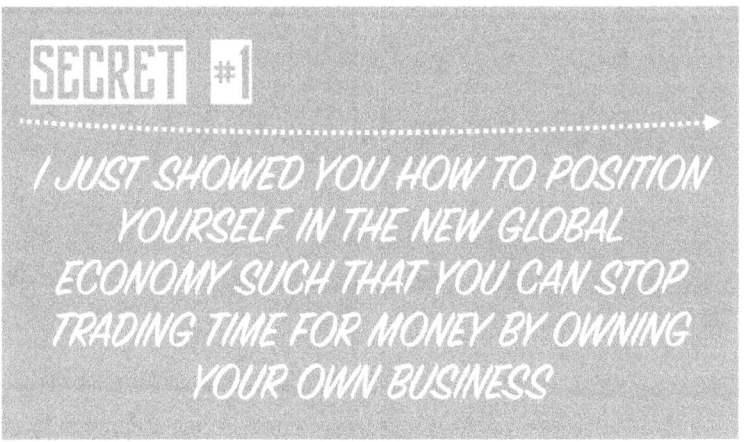

SECRET #1

I JUST SHOWED YOU HOW TO POSITION YOURSELF IN THE NEW GLOBAL ECONOMY SUCH THAT YOU CAN STOP TRADING TIME FOR MONEY BY OWNING YOUR OWN BUSINESS

That said, I just showed you how to not only position yourself in the new global economy *and* stop trading time for money, but I also showed you how to do so by owning your own business and becoming an investor in the success of other businesses.

7. Secret #2 = You Can Earn While You Learn

Earlier in the book I told you my story (chapter 4). And then I shared Ernie's (chapter 5). Remember, we both did *everything* we were told to do– as far as being "responsible" adults. We finished high school, we graduated from college… and we found ourselves– both of us– in massive debt. Neither of us now work in the field we originally pursued while in college.

It's almost as if we followed a bad script. **Yet, as strange as it sounds, it's the story of many of the people I know**.

You know the routine (you might have even done it along with us!):

- Invest 4 years of your time
- Pay $40,000 in tuition fees (or more!) to do it

- Graduate, thereby earning the "right" to look for a job that (you hope) will pay you $40,000 a year

- Work that job for 40 years

- Then… maybe… retire and enjoy the rest of your life (of course, many retirees are now discovering they need to go back to work to earn enough just to meet basic financial obligations)

4 years
$40,000 + paid
For the right one day earn $40K year
For 40 years…
And… maybe… retire and enjoy the rest.

Most people discover that they eventually find themselves in careers that have *nothing* to do with what they learned in college. I'm not against college at all, but I do think we need to be *honest* about how it works: **we can learn a great deal about focus, self-discipline, and spreading our wings while at a four-year institution, but a degree is no guarantee of a future paycheck**.

Furthermore, in the middle of our lives, when were loaded with family and financial responsibilities (i.e., we don't have much extra time or money– we're trapped in that terrible time-for-money tango), we don't have the ability to go back and get a "do over," to re-learn a new skill or trade that we can use now. We can't put life on hold. If we're going to do something new, it's got to get quick results—we've got to earn while we learn and learn while we earn. **Whereas the current "system" suggests you must learn *before* you earn, you can actually do both at the same time.** A legitimate home-based business is the perfect chance to do this– especially when it requires very little cost to "go to market."

(And, remember, it also accomplishes Secret #1, also, allowing you to become a Business Owner and Investor.)

Seven reality checks

I meet people all the time who agree with everything you and I have discussed thus far and *still* come up with (valid) excuses. Notice, I said their excuses are *valid*. That means they're well-founded.

However, most of these people just need more information. Once they receive solid answers, they see the opportunity to "boost" that's before them.

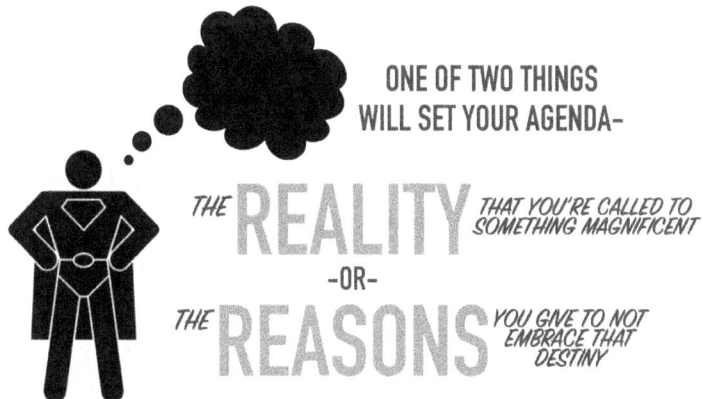

I've learned this. One of two things will set your agenda. Either the reasons you give not to embrace your destiny will set your course, or the reality that you're called to something magnificent will.

So, let's talk through seven of the most common reasons people give– and the reality they (and perhaps you) need to know. We want to let the realities (not the reasons) set our agenda.

Reason #1: *I don't know enough!*

Reality #1: You never know everything you need to know when you begin something new. That's why your current employer trained you. Later, I'll tell you about a few on-ramps our company has. And, this is why you can "earn while you learn." You'll never stop learning.

Reason #2: *I'm too young.*

(Another variation of Reason #2 is *I'm too old!*)

Reality #2: There are people in their 20s and in their 80s who've reached the highest ranks in the company. Regardless of how young or old you are, you still have plenty of years left. The time is going to pass, regardless of whether you do something productive or not. The sooner you get started, the sooner you succeed.

There's an ancient Chinese proverb that asks, "When's the best time to plant a tree?"

The answer... *50 years ago!*

Below is a picture of David Stewart– a pastor I met on an award trip to Ecuador (this is where Young Living has a farm, as well as the Young Living Academy for which my friends raised money to buy that bus we discussed in point 4 of chapter 4). In his 70s, Dr. Stewart led an organization at one of the highest ranks.

Reason #3: *I don't have the time or money, so I can't do this.*

Reality #3: That's why you're still reading this book. You want to break that cycle, jump off the treadmill, and stop time for money and money for time. You realize there's a better way– and that this might very well be it.

Reason #4: *I don't know enough people.*

Reality #4: That's not a problem. In fact, most people don't know that many people (the average person only knows about 200 people, regardless of how many Facebook "friends" it appears that we have).

We use a system that brings people to you. And, it keeps them connected to you once they arrive. We'll talk more about this in Secret #3.

Reason #5: *I'm not outgoing, I'm not a public speaker*, or any version of *I'm an introvert*.

Reality #5: Good. Those things can actually be liabilities in this business, because you might tend to lean on your skillset rather than the system we use. Though you may have certain skills, you want the people you empower towards success to be able to replicate everything you do.

Reason #6: *I don't have enough education*.

Reality #6: This actually works in your favor, too. My experience has been that people who have a lot of education– particularly people with business degrees– don't fair as well in this industry.

Here's why: They can't get beyond the time-for-money tango. They believe that if you've been in an industry for a longer amount of time (i.e., they've been in some sort of business job for decades, sometimes), then you should make more money.

But there's no correlation to how long you've been doing something and how much you make. Your paycheck is a reflection of the value you bring to the market – whether it's a recent addition or not.

In the end, this is a "relationship" business– not a "business" business. If you can get along with people and serve them well, you'll succeed radically. If not, regardless of how many degrees you have and how much you think you're worth, you'll struggle.

Reason #7: *I'm not a leader– or I don't feel like one.*

Reality #7: This might be true, right now. But you'll learn while you earn and you'll earn while you learn. In fact, "personal growth" has proven to be one of my three biggest surprises.

My three biggest surprises

After that pivotal trip to Hawaii, I went "all in" with the "work from home" mindset. I did so primarily for financial reasons– not so that I could earn a million dollars per year but so that I could make enough money to cover the bills and still spend time with my family.

I didn't expect the following to happen– almost as bonuses. But, they've been so incredible that I want to share them with you.

1. **Community**
2. **Personal Growth**
3. **Outlook**

First, community. I've not only been able to travel around the world, both working and having fun with some of the greatest people I've ever met, but I really believe that I could travel any major city in the country at this point and find someone's home where I could stay for the night. When I walked through one of the darkest seasons of my life, it was the group of men whom I met through this business that literally slid in and caught me when I was falling.

How many people can say that about a business?

How many people can even say that about a church or community of faith?

Second, personal growth. One of my biggest surprises was being stretched into new skills. Since I began this business I've written over a dozen books, I've created multiple online courses, and I've spoken at numerous events– large and small.

I've also run a 50-K, climbed Mount Kilimanjaro, and assisted a friend in launching a totally unrelated online business.

Those are not things I *ever* planned to do. Nor did I know *how* to do any of them before my venture into network marketing. But, I attribute each of those experiences to doors which opened because of this opportunity.

This is a picture of men speaking at an event in Nashville…

And here is a picture of me onstage in Dallas.

Quite simply, this business has offered me consistent invitations to express who I was created to be.

Third, my outlook. I tell you this, too– the way I view my week transformed. I've always been a positive person, but I loved making it to Fridays and being able to hit the "pause" button for a few days. After a 60-80 hour grind, I needed the break.

Don't get me wrong. I still enjoy the weekends. I like seeing family, doing big projects around the house, and going on long runs and bike rides while there's less traffic. But, I actually look forward to the workweek as well.

> **I'm grateful for the weekend, but I look forward to the workweek.**

In other words, this entire "earn while you learn" and "learn while you earn" scenario doesn't just mean a larger paycheck (that is, my external factors changed), but it has resulted in a "new me" at the same time (that is, my internal factors changed). I like to say it this way: **This business opportunity is not just about what you achieve, it's who you become in the process.**

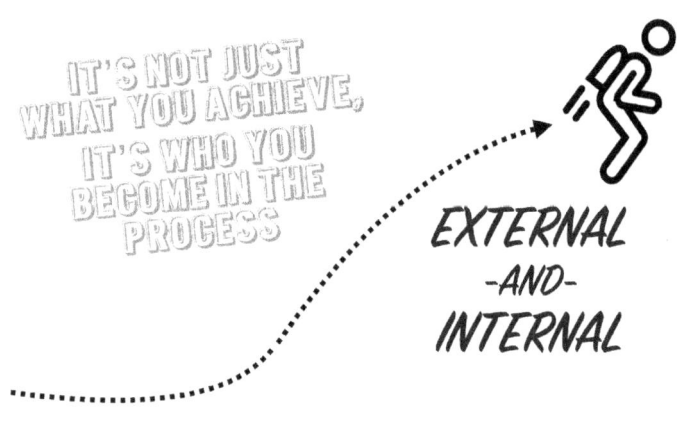

Road map

Earlier, I told you that you could "earn while you learn" and "learn while you earn." And, more importantly, you can do it even if you don't have a lot of extra time or money. In fact, those are the two issues we're trying to resolve– most of us need more time and we need more money.

In the Spring 2020 our company created two new incentive programs, *Silver Bound* and *Bridge to Gold*. Both of these programs help new distributors "pace" their way towards higher ranks in the company, while incentivizing them along the way.

Here's the problem, though. And it seems counter-intuitive. **The investment cost for you to enter the market is so low that many people don't take the opportunity seriously. And, when people invest "just a little" to get started in a business, they tend to undervalue it**. When the entry cost is higher, people tend to want to recoup that investment.

A year ago, Ernie and Jim Bob, two of the guys I work with, flew to Young Living's new global headquarters to meet with several of the executives and shoot some film.

When we met Sarah, the head of U.S. Sales, she actually exclaimed, "I can't believe more people aren't doing this!" Then– "I mean, the entry cost is so low!"

She ranted (graciously) about how people don't have to maintain inventory, how they spend less to enter this legitimate business than they often do in purchasing a single pair of shoes and uniform-clothes for minimum wage jobs at fast food restaurants, and how there are copious amounts of training videos and written resources available for them– all created by other people who are incentivized to help them succeed.

"Plus, they can *earn while they learn*," she said.

"I know," I concurred. "I'm putting that in our next book. *Learn while you earn*– and *earn while you learn*."

She added, "Tell them that **they at least deserve to take a look at the data for themselves and see what it could mean for them and their family.**"

Despite her access to all of this info, my cousin joined a *different* network marketing company. She quit a few months later, after spending thousands of dollars on products, on training, and on marketing resources.

Our company only encourages you to buy products you were already purchasing anyway (I explain this in Secret #3), we provide free training (by people who are paid bonuses to empower you to succeed– and only paid after you do), and we provide you with great marketing resources *free of charge*.

Plus, we often send people who are seriously considering this as a business another book we wrote, *Flight*, which explains the compensation plan in super-simple and pleasantly practical language. It shows them exactly how long it should take to hit various ranks in the company, what income levels they should expect, and how to leverage their time so that they do "income-producing activities" rather than simply doing "busy work."

(We call it *Flight* because we want to help you launch your business and propel it to higher levels.)

Right now, you might find yourself in the position any of these other people I've worked with before found themselves.

- Stephanie was a stay-at-home mom who just had a baby and wanted to find a creative way to earn extra income and improve her family's bottom line without going back to work.

She hosted a few classes and now earns about $600 per month working ultra-part-time.

- Erin was a new mom and a busy full-time beautician at a local salon when she first pursued this opportunity.

  She still cuts hair about 30 hours per week and loves it, but she earns more (about $4,000 per month, almost double what she makes from her "day job") with this "side hustle."

- April (an entrepreneur and small business owner) had never been to a class about our products before.

  She hosted a class and made $400 her first night. The second evening she earned over $1,000. Within eight months, she was earning $10,000 per month.

REAL PEOPLE

Stephanie — STAY AT HOME MOM. JUST HAD A BABY
$600 / month, residual income

Erin — BUSY MOM, FULL-TIME
$4,000 / month, residual income - within one year!

April — HAD NEVER BEEN TO A CLASS
$400 IN ONE NIGHT! $1,000+ THE SECOND NIGHT
$10,000+ each month!

That leads me to a few questions. Take some time to consider them and even write your answers in the margins of the book.

- What would your life look like with an extra $2,000 – $5,000 per month?

- What about $10,000 per month?

- What if, like April, it only took you just over half a year to make that happen?

- What if it took a few years?

These are real people.

The reality isn't lost on me that when you support a home-based business you aren't funding another vacation home, a new sports car, or a second yacht. You're helping people pay for their kids' braces, spend more time at home rather than chasing work in order to pay the mortgage, and empowering normal people like you and me to live their best life now.

Furthermore, I'm aware that when I help people launch a new business which attains those results, I'm encouraging, equipping, and empowering them to do the exact same thing.

WHAT WOULD YOUR LIFE LOOK LIKE WITH $2,000– $5,000 OR MORE EXTRA / MONTH?

WHAT IF IT TOOK A FEW YEARS?

WHAT IF IT ONLY TOOK YOU A FEW MONTHS?

People often ask me, "How long did it take you to reach a $10,000 per month income?"

The answer… a year. It occurred the same month we achieved the rank of Platinum (you might recognize a similar graphic from the point 3 in chapter 4), a significant biz building rank in Young Living.

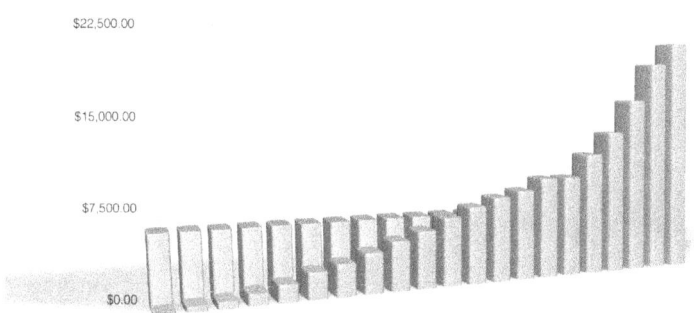

People *also* often ask me, "What keeps people from succeeding?"

Or– "Is there a consistent factor whereby you know they won't make it?"

Turns out, there is. And here it is. **Some people simply quit too soon**.

Take a look at the picture on the following page and ask yourself, "Who is closer to reaching their goal?"

Technically, the man on the bottom is *closer*. Yet, at the same time, he isn't. He's facing the wrong direction.

The "earn while you learn" and "learn while you earn" system we have is a proven process. And **if you continue stepping– and chipping away– in the right**

direction, you *will* reap results. This is your vehicle. The training you need– which empowers you to learn while you earn– will help you attain a (growing) residual income. Just like we discussed in point 1 of chapter 3.

In other words, I just showed you how you can earn while you learn (a significant income), even if you have little or no skills in this industry.

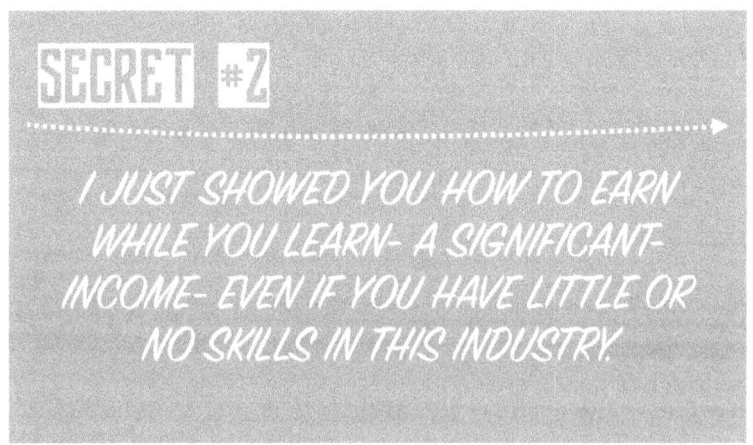

SECRET #2

I JUST SHOWED YOU HOW TO EARN WHILE YOU LEARN- A SIGNIFICANT-INCOME- EVEN IF YOU HAVE LITTLE OR NO SKILLS IN THIS INDUSTRY.

8. Secret #3 = You Can Do It Without Selling Stuff...

Two chapters ago, we studied Robert Kiyosaki's Four Quadrants (he's the author of *Rich Dad, Poor Dad*) and decided that we've got to become a Business Owner (top right) and an Investor (bottom right) instead of an Employee (top left) or even Self-Employed (bottom left). I proposed the best way to achieve that was through network marketing, a methodology Kiyosaki himself endorses.

The business model is really an *external* factor– it's something *outside* of you.

In the previous chapter, I observed that despite the fact that we might be young or old, that we might have a little or a lot of education, regardless of whether we know many people or just a few, and irrelevant of how under-qualified or over-qualified we might think we are (I offered seven reasons people use to overlook reality), I proposed that– again– network marketing provides that vehicle for us to "earn while we learn" and "learn while we earn."

In other words, this model helps us overcome *internal* factors— issues related *to us.*

In this chapter, I want to dive deeper and discuss the vehicle itself. You see, one of the biggest (and baddest) stereotypes people have about network marketing is that in order to succeed you'll have to sell a whole bunch of things that–

1. People don't want

2. People don't need

3. People don't know how to use

4. People won't ever use

If that was true, that would mean that (just match the numbers below to the points above)–

1. You'll have to push people to get the sell (because they don't want what you have)

2. You'll have a bunch of products people don't typically want, thereby making it even more difficult to sell (people don't know how to use them, because those products are abnormal to the regular routine of life)

3. The product is an exclusive item or an elite purchase and will have a high price point, requiring lots of convincing (people can't afford it, so most of yours sales will be "pity purchases" and will require lots of begging and emotional manipulation)

4. You'll have to continue finding new customers in order to keep the income stream coming (people buy once and are done, and they'll likely hide form you the next time they see you coming)

What if there's a better way?

What if I could show you a business model whereby you don't have to "recruit people" but (instead) they came seeking you?

What if I could show you an industry that is recession proof– something that is so intricately interwoven into the fabric of people's lives such that it will always (not matter how great or how tough things got) will always be around?

What if I could show you something that people will purchase over and over, again and again, because it is something they were already buying anyway?

I bet that would capture your interest!

People always take care of themselves

Experts forecast that the personal care industry will reach $650 billion by the year 2024– just a few years away. About $25 billion of that will be environmentally friendly or organic.

GLOBAL PERSONAL CARE BY 2024

$650 BILLION
$25 BILLION SPECIFICALLY "GREEN"

"Personal care" includes all the activities we do to groom and nurture ourselves–including everything from protein shakes and supplements to toothpaste and deodorant to ways we choose to manage stress.

Think about the products *many* (not *most*, but *many*) people use every single day. These include:

- Vitamins, supplements, hormone support
- Energy drinks, energy bars
- Fitness + recovery
- Weight loss products / weight management
- Outdoor products, such as insect repellant and sunscreen
- Other household products, like scents and cleaners
- Laundry
- Pet care

*ITEMS **MANY** USE EVERY DAY*

- VITAMINS, SUPPLEMENTS, HORMONE SUPPORT
- ENERGY DRINKS, ENERGY BARS
- FITNESS + RECOVERY
- WEIGHT LOSS PRODUCTS / WEIGHT MANAGEMENT
- OUTDOOR PRODUCTS- LIKE INSECT REPELLENT + SUNSCREEN
- OTHER HOUSEHOLD- LIKE SCENTS, CLEANERS
- LAUNDRY
- PET CARE

In addition, think about the products that *most* (not just *many*, but *most*) people use every day–

- Personal products (shower, shave, lotion, etc.)
- Household products (soap, dishwashing, etc.)
- Toothpaste, floss, mouthwash
- Deodorant, cologne / perfume
- Skin care + beauty
- Make up

*ITEMS **MOST** PEOPLE USE EVERY DAY*

- PERSONAL CARE PRODUCTS (SHOWER, SHAVE, LOTION, ETC.)
- HOUSEHOLD PRODUCTS- SOAP, DISHWASHING, ETC.
- TOOTHPASTE, FLOSS, MOUTH WASH
- DEODORANT, COLOGNE / PERFUME
- SKIN CARE + BEAUTY
- MAKE UP

When you create a business built around these products, you *don't* have to sell any of the following–

1. Products people don't want
2. Products people don't need

3. Products people don't know how to use

4. Products people won't ever use

You may recognize those four as the categories we admitted we want to *avoid* just a few pages ago.

But what if the economy turns down?

The fascinating thing about these products is that they're recession-proof. Recently, our entire nation– even the entire world– shut down with the Covid-19 crisis. Regardless of your opinion as to how this was handled politically or with (or without) ulterior motives, here are a few of the things that occurred:

- School was cancelled– yes, cancelled– for the remaining two months of the year (Seniors were considered "graduated" with over 8 weeks of class remaining).

- Self-distancing measures, whereby people wouldn't step within 6-feet of one another, were on the rise.

- Tape on the floors at checkout counters in grocery stores and other retailers helped distance shoppers (that precious 6-feet) from one another.

- Stores limited the number of people allowed inside (i.e., Home Depot allowed only 100 at a time), thereby creating lineups outside the stores.

- Non-essential stores and businesses were mandated *closed* (the government exercised unprecedented power to declare which businesses were "essential" and then close movie theaters, department stores, and even limited restaurants to curbside pickup and delivery).

- Many parks and trails closed.

- Entire professional sports seasons were cancelled.

- Concerts, tours, festivals, entertainment events were cancelled.

- Weddings, family celebrations, holiday gatherings were experienced via Zoom, Facetime, or other forms of video chat.

- No masses or church services were allowed– including Easter celebrations.

- No gatherings of 50 or more, then 20 or more, then 10 or more were allowed.

- You weren't permitted to socialize with anyone outside of your home.

- There was a shortage of masks, gowns, and gloves for our front-line health workers.

- There was a shortage of ventilators for the critically ill.

- Manufacturers, distilleries and other businesses switched their assembly lines to help produce visors, masks, hand sanitizer, and PPE.

- Our government closed the border to all non-essential travel.

- Fines as high as $500 (and even imprisonment with a misdemeanor conviction) were established for breaking the rules.

- Stadiums, recreation facilities, and parking decks– not being used for their regular fares, because of the shutdown– opened for the overflow of Covid-19 patients.

- The President of the United States delivered *daily* press conferences. He updated the American people on the new cases, the recent deaths, and the recovery totals.

- The roads were bare.

- Many people wore masks and gloves outside of their homes– and even scuttled to move away from strangers in the aisle in the grocery stories.

- Essential service workers (the government deemed healthcare workers and other specific industries as "essential," whereas professional athletes, actors, and others we routinely admire were hardly mentioned at all) were terrified to go to work. At the same time, those *same* medical field workers who might have been exposed all day were *also* afraid to go home to their families.

And here are two additional happenings which relate directly to our proposed "boost" scenario:

- **Panic buying set in.** We ran out of toilet paper and paper towels, disinfecting supplies, laundry soap, and hand sanitizer. Though there was plenty of ice cream, alcohol, and snack foods to be purchased, **the shelves were barren of personal care products.**

- Despite many people no longer having a job (or being furloughed until stores were permitted to re-open), everyone continued taking baths, brushing their teeth, cleaning their homes, and working on their mental and emotional health. In fact, **personal care become *more important* during this season than at any other time.** As luxuries and preferences were allowed to go... people clung to the necessities, that is, personal care products.

Again, people always take care of themselves– even when they stop buying cars, purchasing new homes, and taking vacations. Or, to say it another way, they postponed the interior-designer but they continued calling the plumber.

Notice the truths presented in the following graphic:

PERSONAL CARE PRODUCTS ARE ALL RECESSION-PROOF, AND THE MARKET WILL NEVER "BE SATURATED"

* BECAUSE MORE PEOPLE CONTINUE BEING BORN

* BECAUSE THE PRODUCTS ARE CONSUMABLE
VS. BOOKS, HAIRBRUSHES

* BECAUSE THE PRODUCTS ARE INEXPENSIVE
VS. KIRBY + OTHER VACUUM CLEANERS

* BECAUSE THE PRODUCTS ARE NOT LUXURY ITEMS
VS. PURSES, PRESS-ON NAILS, ETC.

* BECAUSE THE PRODUCTS ARE THINGS PEOPLE ALREADY USE

All of that (in my thinking) means this: if you can show people where they can find healthier versions of these items *now* (which they can continue purchasing when tough times come), they'll know where to go later– *whether times or good or bad.* They'll have a supplier ready to meet that need. And it won't cost them more money to do it.

Because people use "budget dollars" rather than disposable income for personal care products, we sometimes refer to these items as one of the following:

- **"replacement products"** (they replace what they were buying from the store with something they can purchase online and have shipped to them),

- **"transfer buys"** (swap what they were grabbing off the shelves and have them sent to the front door), *or simply*

- **"budget dollars"** (because the money was already dedicated to a specific cost)

MONEY YOU + OTHERS ALREADY SPEND

* PEOPLE CAN BUY MORE W/OUT SPENDING MORE
* SOMETIMES CALLED...
  - REPLACEMENT PRODUCTS
  - SWAP BUYS
  - TRANSFER BUYS
* BETTER FOR YOUR BIZ GROWTH!

Do you remember what I promised you at the beginning of this chapter?

I said we can do this without making people buy stuff they don't want, don't need, don't know how to use, or won't ever use. Everyone is *already* brushing their teeth, cleaning their house, doing their laundry, and trying to live well– every single day. When you open a "store" that carries superior versions of these items (always healthier, and often at a much lower cost), people come asking for more.

(This also fits well with those two global trends we discussed in point #4 of chapter 3 about direct shopping and low start up costs!)

How we do it

A few years ago, I posted my "shopping hack" on social media. I included a graphic and a small write-up.

Here's what I communicated…

Once a month, Mini (= my nickname for my then 7 year old, Miriam) and I used to drive to Costco to purchase a month's worth of goods. For a house of eleven people. She rode with me, because the other kids are loud *and* Mini is my "Tetris" packer (remember that game?!). As we walked through the store, grabbing only the items we required, Mini always set the boxes facing up, insuring we could move through checkout quickly (the store employees were always baffled that my little girl packed us so efficiently and that we required very little assistance).

Sometimes we acquired a flatbed cart and an over-sized shopping buggy by the time we finished our loop through the big box store. Here's how we made it work in the Volkswagen Jetta (which my then 4 year old, Salter, referred to as the "tiny car."). Mini and I bought some of the things we couldn't get cheaper anywhere else. Things like milk, eggs, bread, cereal… fruit, veggies.

As I checked-out I always sent Mini to the in-store cafe with my debit card. I handled payment while she grabbed her prize– a "berry blast" ice cream sundae.

From there, we let Young Living shipping *everything else* to us (this is, in truth, the only way we were able to toss a month's worth of shopping for 11 people into a small vehicle). Even though Costco carries many of the other *kinds* of items we regularly use, and even though Mini and I drove past at least a dozen other retailers where we could pick them up, we ordered them online and had Young Living ship them to us.

Here's why:

- Young Living's products are top-of-the-line in each of the categories.

- Young Living's products are, usually, less expensive than what I grab at big box retailers.

- Young Living's products arrive at my front door (no weaving through a warehouse, no packing the cart, no checkout, no loading my car, no toting from the car to the house).

- Young Living's products come at 24% off retail (for wholesale members) and we earn 25% back in points towards free items we choose (as members of their no-cost, non-obligatory frequent buyer program, known as Essential Rewards).

- Young Living's business opportunity supports my family's and many other families' small business and, therefore, their livelihood.

Shopping at Costco meant a one-hour round trip, a two-hour ramble through the store (which was enjoyable, because it was quality time with Mini), but we received nothing (except the in-store samples) for free. And we had to find our own boxes.

Shopping with Young Living meant– and means– a few clicks on the computer, huge discounts, and free products. And, it's the vehicle we use to live and work from anywhere, pursue the live of our dreams, and escape that time-for-money tango. (There's no ice cream involved, but the time-and-money freedom give us plenty of margin to head to the local shoppe.)

Notice the graphic above— the one I posted online. **Look at the items on the list. They aren't obscure. They're items I buy anyway— every single month.** When the economy is up and when it's down.

The only difference between the products I order online and the products I used to purchase at the store is that—

- I purchase higher quality products from Young Living than I could ever find at the supermarket, the corner store, or the big box

- I save money— the price is often significantly cheaper

- I use their super-cheap shipping features (even when I pay a little, the shipping cost is still cheaper than the gas I would use driving across town— it still frazzles me that some people complain about paying for shipping)

- I receive free products every month through some of the Monthly Promos they run

- I always earn points— on every purchase— towards other products I can choose on my own, when I'm ready

As much as I love Costco (and shopping with Mini, plus grabbing an under-priced, over-sized sundae), Young Living's set up beats theirs every single time.

People often ask, "What does Young Living have? What can you get there?"

When I say "just about everything except milk, bread, meat, and toilet paper," that's what I mean. They have 500+ essential oil-infused products in their inventory (which means they have enough of a selection for everyone to find something they need– something they would already purchase from somewhere anyway).

A quick fly-over

On the following pages, I'll show you a few things I order online. My purpose isn't to show you *everything*– it's just to highlight *some* of the things and illustrate the expansive nature of the offerings. I bet you already purchase most of these items, anyway– meaning your friends and family and co-workers do, too. And, **I bet you and most of the people you know continue buying many of these items even in times of economic uncertainty.**

Let me pull back the curtain.

Here's another series of graphics I used on social media a few years ago, an image that provided several categories of products we carry— all designed to demonstrate where people can begin dumping toxins from their home. (We've even mentioned that alone as a huge reason to delve into this industry— people are looking for chemical free. That's why the boy on the top right has his nose clipped— toxins!)

6 PLACES TO START
ELIMINATING TOXINS TODAY!

Personal Care Products b/c you should haven't to choose between looking good vs. your health
Vitamins & Supplements b/c supplements should infuse you with health instead of garbage
Cleaning Supplies b/c your cleaning supplies should actually be "clean"
Negative Thinking + Stress b/c it's easier to control what happens "in here" than stuff "out there"
Scents & Smells b/c you should experience beauty of your senses without the bite of toxins
Faux Essential Oils b/c you & your family deserve something authentic and pure

One of the first areas of personal care (the top item on my list in the image above) is for ladies to take a quick look at their bathroom cabinet.

BEAUTY + SKIN

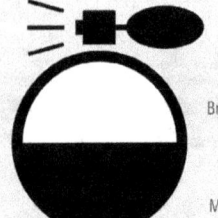

Facewash ART Gentle Cleanser (5361)
Toner ART Refreshing Toner (5360)
Moisturizer ART Light Moisturizer (5362)
Eye cream Wolfberry Eye Cream (5145)
Brightener cream Sheerlume (4833)
Makeup Savvy Minerals (various)
Deodorant Mountain Mist Deodorant (3753)
Lotion Hand & Body Lotion (5201)
Makeup remover YL Seedlings Baby Wipes (20428)

I tell everyone to take a look in the men's cabinet, as well. Many people forget that one of the most rapidly-growing subsets of personal care is men's products. Do a quick search online and you'll find everything from shaving-kit clubs to men's grooming boxes to personal shopping designed just for men.

Bodywash	Shutran 3-in-1 Men's Wash (20483)
Beard	Shutran Beard Oil (19802)
No Beard	Shutran Shave Cream (5157) + Shutran Aftershave (5710)
Healthy testosterone	Idaho Blue Spruce essential oil (3093)
Goldenrod (self-explanatory)	Goldenrod essential oil (3562)
Prostate + Reproductive Health	Mister essential oil (3381)
Immune Support + Physical Stamina + Mental Clarity	PowerGize supplement (4748)

Of course, many of us have children in the home, as well as and products designed specifically for them. Finding healthy alternatives we can trust has become more important lately, particularly as many once-trusted vendors have revealed holes (and even cover-ups) in their supply chain.

Baby Lotion	YL Seedlings Calm Scent (20438)
Baby Oil	YL Seedlings Calm Scent (20373)
Baby Wipes	YL Seedlings Calm Scent (20428)
Diaper Cream	YL Seedlings Diaper Rash Cream (20398)
Kids' Shampoo	KidScents Shampoo (3686)
Kids' Bodywash	KidScents Bath Gel (3684)
Kids' Lotion	KidScents Slique Toothpaste (4574)
Wellness Kit	KidScents Oils Collection
Kids' Multivitamins	Kids' MightyVites Chewables (20557)
Kids' Diffusers	Dolphin (5333), Dino (5332), Horse (5490)

After that Hawaii trip I lost 50-pounds. While doing so I leaned heavily on the protein shakes from Young Living as part of my meal plan.

Healthy weight management Slique Shake (5552)
Meal replacement Balance Complete (3292)
Muscle + protein Pure Protein Vanilla (3301) or Chocolate (3298)

And, a few years ago, right as I began that endeavor, Walmart and GNC revealed that many of their products were intentionally mislabeled. Thankfully, I had already found healthier– pure– alternatives before any of the information surfaced.

Immune Support NingXia Red (3042)
Daily multi-vitamin Master Formula (5292)
Green supplement MultiGreens (3248)
Seasonal Support Allerzyme (3288)
Joint Health AgilEase (5764)
Brain & heart health MindWise (4747)
Probiotic Life 9 (18299)
Hormone support Progressence Plus Serum (4640)
Fish oil OmegaGize (3097)
Digestive support Essentialzyme (3272)

Now, whereas many people don't purchase protein shakes and supplements, the vast majority of people I know clean their house, their vehicles, and their "stuff."

CLEANING

Floor cleaner — Thieves Household Cleaner (3743)
Carpet cleaner — Thieves Household Cleaner (3743)
Dusting / dust spray — Thieves Household Cleaner (3743)
Mirror / window spray — Thieves Household Cleaner (3743)
Toilet /bathroom cleaner — Thieves Household Cleaner (3743)
Cleaning wipes — Thieves Wipes (3756)
Air freshener — Diffuser of your choice + essential oils

Again, these are all dollars people are accustomed to spending every month anyway. There is no learning curve in order to use the products, nor do people have to "save up" for them. They're already spending the money.

KITCHEN

Dish soap — Thieves Dish Soap (5350)
Hand soap — Thieves Foaming Hand Soap (3674)
Dish detergent — Thieves Dishwasher Powder (5762)
Counter spray — Thieves Household Cleaner (3743)

The kitchen, the laundry room, and the bathroom are some of the most utilitarian rooms in the home. (And they're one of the places you'll find the most toxins).

BATHROOM

Bodywash	Bath & Shower Gel (3751) + oil of your choice
Shampoo	Lavender Shampoo (5100)
Facewash	Orange Blossom Facial Wash (5136)
Toothpaste	Thieves AromaBright Toothpaste (3039)
Mouthwash	Thieves Fresh Essence (3683)
Dental Floss	Thieves Dental Floss (4464122)
Body Lotion	Lavender Hand & Body Lotion (5201)
Body Butter	Coconut Lime Body Butter (20225)
Air freshener	Diffuser of your choice + Purification oil
Toilet + mirrors	Thieves Household Cleaner (3743)

Here are a few additional categories which interest many people...

NEGATIVE THINKING + STRESS

Sleep Emotional Release	Freedom Sleep & Release Bundle (9869)
Positive Thinking	Oola Infused Seven Kit (5058)
Negativity shield	White Angelica essential oil (3432)
Empowerment	Believe essential oil (4661)

And then there are scents and candles– each of which have been determined to be loaded with carcinogens.

SCENTS + SMELLS

Room freshener Diffuser of your choice + oils of your choice
Diffuser with night light Dew Drop Diffuser (5330)
Contemporary design diffuser Desert Mist Diffuser (21558)
Minimalist design diffuser Rainstone Diffuser (5331)
Art deco design diffuser Aria Difuser (4524)
Personal diffuser Gentle Mist Personal Diffuser Set (22907)
Computer / workspace USB personal diffuser (multiple colors- 5224)
Kids' Diffusers Dolphin (5333), Dino (5332), Horse (5490)

* Replace candles, plug-ins, aerosol sprays, fragrance sticks with the above

And, of course, there is the pro-active side of things.

PRO-ACTIVE HEALTH

Sunscreen Mineral Sunscreen Lotion (20667)
Bug Repellant Insect Repellant (20701)
Cough Drops Thieves Cough Drops (5759)
Pain Cream Cool Azul Pain Cream (5759)
Energy Boosters NingXia Nitro (3064)
Total Body Infusion NingXia Red (3042)
Daily Multi-Vitamin Master Formula (5292)

Throughout this book I've conveyed that **you can do this business without pushing people to buy things they don't want, they don't need, they don't know how to use, they won't ever use... or they can't afford.** In this chapter I've shown you how you can grow a business (long-term) without hassling people. In fact, they'll continue ordering because they *already* purchase these things. You'll show them a better place to purchase better products at a better price.

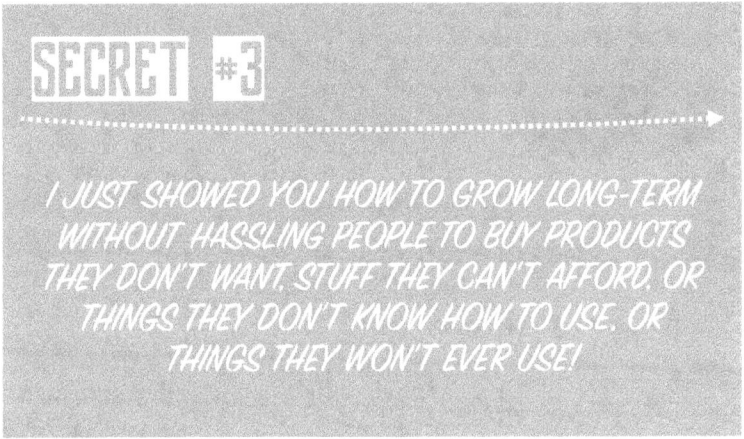

That's a wrap

As we conclude our discussion of the three secrets that *they* don't want you to know, think back to our two premises in chapter 2:

1. **The best (not the *only*, but the *best*) way to change your financial outlook is by becoming a network marketing**

professional. Yes, there are other ways to do it– and people do it all the time. This isn't the *only* way, but this is the *best* way.

2. **The best (not the *only*, but the *best*) way to "do" network marketing is with Young Living Essential Oils**, the company with which I'm affiliated (again, there are other ways to do network marketing, but my biased opinion is that this is the *best* way).

MY GOAL = SHOW YOU >>>

THE BEST WAY TO STOP TRADING
TIME FOR MONEY IS THROUGH
NETWORK MARKETING, AND

THE BEST WAY TO DO NETWORK
MARKETING IS WITH YOUNG LIVING!

IF I SHOW YOU THAT THIS IS TRUE,
YOU'LL WANT TO WORK WITH US...

This leads us to the final part of our journey together, "The Real Question."

8. SECRET #3 = YOU CAN DO IT WITHOUT SELLING STUFF...

Part 3 = The Real Question

9. If / Then

Over the past 150 pages I've given you *a lot* of information…

- We've been raw and real– and decided a "do-over" is probably long over-due (chapter 1).

- We've talked about the time-for-money tango– and how that villain gets the best of us, even if we're not motivated by money (chapter 2).

- We discussed four mindset shifts we've got to make, and learned that the most likely path to freedom is (ironically) the only pyramid which people (wrongly) accuse of being a scheme (chapter 3).

- I shared my story (chapter 4) and Ernie offered his (chapter 5), explaining that even though we did "everything right" we still got bad results (confirming the suspicions we outlined in chapter 1).

- After that, we talked about the three secrets…

Now, my three-fold question to you is this:

- If you tap into the concepts I relayed in Secret #1, and stop trading time for money and become a Business Owner and Investor instead…

- If you *earn while you learn* and *learn while you earn*, like we discussed in Secret #2, as opposed to waiting until you graduate four years from now (if you even have the time and money to go back to school)– and are able to earn a growing income even if you don't have experience in the industry…

- If you actually do this, like we outlined in Secret #3, without hassling people to purchase products they don't want, don't know how to use, don't need, and won't ever want to repurchase– and, in fact, they come to you begging to buy more (even in times of economic uncertainty)…

… *if you do each of these three things, then will this work for you?*

The answer is, emphatically, "Yes, this will work for you!"

THEN THE ANSWER IS…

YES, THIS WILL WORK FOR YOU!

By implementing this system, you will be able to work from anywhere + live the life of your dreams. You'll find yourself escaping the 9-5, living well, doing the most good, and bringing others on the journey with you.

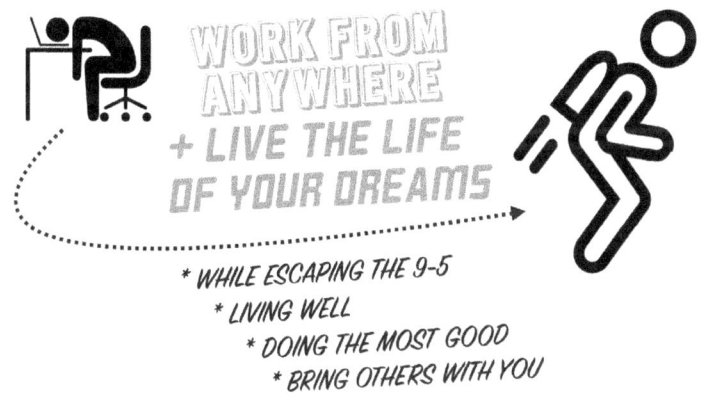

Here's why. A reliable system creates a two-fold on-ramp for you, whereby you can immediately implement the following:

1. **The process.** You'll learn while you earn and earn while you learn, thereby knowing what to do (and what not to do) in order to succeed. That is, you'll understand the business model and the industry.

2. **The products.** You'll learn the company's inventory. You'll understand which "replacement products" to direct people towards.

Over the next few pages I'll outline two tools we have to empower you in each of these areas.

1. The process = how to do the biz

About four months after going "all in" with the business, April– one our downline team members– reached out for help. I mentioned her in chapter 7, when I discussed Secret #2 and talked about real people earning while they continued learning.

"We have a bunch of people up here wanting to do the business," she said, "but we're not sure how to explain it. It's all new to us."

We were thrilled to assist them, because their success was / is our success. (Remember, network marketing works differently than typical business– your upline *wants* to work for you and empower you.)

"What exactly do you need?"

"Well, we've got a good handle on the products," she replied. "I mean, we're learning more every day, but we're definitely moving in the right direction there. We need help deciphering the compensation plan, a few tips on how to best get business builders started, we need to point them to a few resources… those sorts of things."

"Gotcha. I think we can help with that!"

We put a date on the calendar, and this dynamic leader began inviting people to attend a Friday evening workshop.

I decided that rather than spewing a bunch of info at people and having them feverishly write down everything they could, I would make it *easy*. So, I created workbooks with fill-in-the-blank answers (and put the answers in the back of the book). I made slides to match the presentation. And I recorded the audio for people who weren't able to attend.

The following image highlights six of the modules I created for those team members:

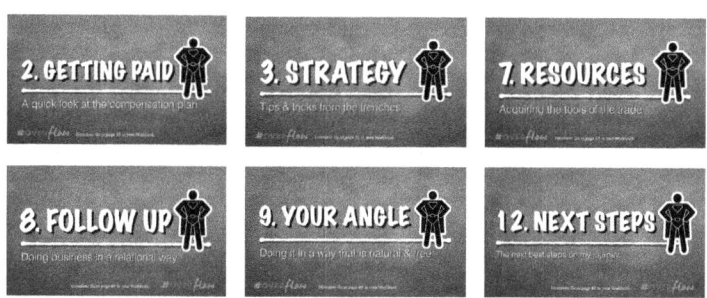

The result is that the majority of the business builders in that relational circle accelerated through the first few ranks. Some of them began earning $3,000 or more within just a few months. (Furthermore, *none* of them had every worked in this industry before. They were all "earning while learning.")

One gal, Amy, hit a significant milestone in the company *in just 9 days*. At the time the company was running a special bonus for people who hit that mark within 6 months. So, between chasing her twins around the house and shuttling the other half of her kids between sports practices and school, she squeezed in some strategic work and got things done.

I texted her back on a group chat, half-kidding, and exclaimed, "You had 6 months to do this– not 6 days!"

(At the time, the average paycheck at that rank was $2,227 per month– and she continued growing, topping $10,000 per month just 6 months later.)

Many of those new business builders were able to rank up *faster* than we had. You see, **they were able to learn from both the successes and failures we shared with them**.

I tell people that module 3– about business strategy– is worth *thousands* of dollars alone. That sounds like an overstatement, I know, but here's my rationale...

MODULE 3, "STRATEGY," IS WORTH THOUSANDS OF DOLLARS ALONE.

IF WE WOULD HAVE STRUCTURED OUR ORGANIZATION DIFFERENTLY IN THE BEGINNING WE WOULD HAVE MADE $1,000s MORE IN BONUSES- PER MONTH.

LEARN FROM OUR MISTAKES!

If we had structured our business a bit differently (just slightly so), we would have hit a higher rank– even with the same business volume– much faster. We would have achieved that higher rank over four years sooner.

- A higher rank would have meant an approximately $1,500 bonus per month– every month for that entire four year period (yes, that's about a $72,000 swing)!

- A higher rank would have meant an all-expenses-paid award trip— just like that Hawaii trip— once per year!

- A higher rank would have meant several other perks, too, such as increased access to corporate support, earlier info on new product launches, and more!

No sense in fretting about it. The best thing to do is to gather the info, fail forward, and empower others with better info to succeed faster— especially when their success is our success!

About six months after teaching this material that first time (and after communicating it to several other groups), I hired a friend and we filmed it. Now, the workshop is available online.

THIS COURSE IS PERFECT FOR

STAY-AT-HOME DADS   ACCOUNTANTS   GRANDMOTHERS
SOCCER MOMS   BIZ OWNERS   PASTORS   TEACHERS
CEOs   RETIREES   COLLEGE STUDENTS   DREAMERS

Will that course help you?

Of course it will. That's why **I *always* make the info available to new team members who want to understand– and then implement– some of the best business practices**. I offer it to them in both video and audio formats.

(This course is also in the online library for all OilyApp+ members. Just login at OilyApp.com. If you want more info on this course, titled *Overflow*, go to OilyApp.com/Overflow.)

2. The products = our biz is built around these

Back in Secret #3, I showed you how to build a business that's recession proof and doesn't require you to beg people to make a purchase (chapter 8). You recognized most of the products I mentioned during those few pages. But, you probably don't yet know the Young Living better counterparts for many of the popular brands.

(And with over 500 SKUs in the inventory, there's no way to memorize them all.)

Here's a great solution. About a year ago, I created a 6-page "Ditch & Switch" worksheet to empower people to know which products to order– and which products to refer to others. I wanted to equip people with a tool that arms people with info– even as they continue learning.

The document works like this: if you know how to use _____ (insert the name of the product you normally use), then you know how to use _____ (the Young Living switch).

So, you...

1. Choose a category in column 1 (i.e., kids, personal care, men, supplements, kitchen, etc.)

2. Find what you usually purchase in column 2

3. Discover the Young Living equivalent in column 3

Our team worked hard to make this tool super-simple and pleasantly practical.

(You can download this worksheet at OilyApp.com/ditchNswitch-- the URL is case-sensitive! And, since the first release of this book we've released an entire paperback about the "Ditch and Switch" process. Learn more at OilyApp.com/switch.)

Sure, we have plenty of other resources available, too– but those *two* are some of the best places to begin. They empower you to start earning an income immediately, because they equip you with the info you need to move from the "I don't know enough to get started" mindset to the "I *do* know enough– I'll start right away and I'll learn more as a continue building my business."

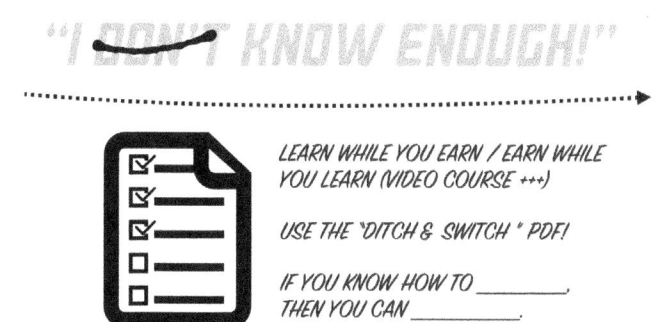

You're not alone

By the way, we never leave anyone dangling on their own. We've created incredible support groups where you can learn more about the products and the business. Our goal is to remove barriers and, at the same time, create launching pads.

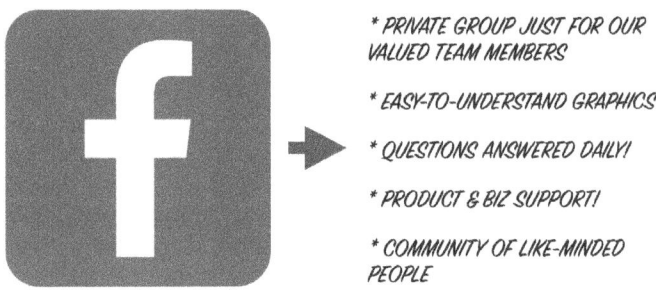

* PRIVATE GROUP JUST FOR OUR VALUED TEAM MEMBERS

* EASY-TO-UNDERSTAND GRAPHICS

* QUESTIONS ANSWERED DAILY!

* PRODUCT & BIZ SUPPORT!

* COMMUNITY OF LIKE-MINDED PEOPLE

We endeavor to create a culture where the question is never, "Can this work for me?"

We want that issue settled, so that they only question that remains is, "Am I willing to invest the time and effort it takes to escape the time-for-money tango?"

If that's the case, then this might very well be your open door to a life of more. Or, to say it another way, **this might be your personal jetpack to maneuver your way towards the life you've dreamed of**.

10. This *Might Be* Your Jetpack

From in the beginning of this book, we talked about the time-for-money tango. We said we desperately want to break free of those shackles, so that we can live the life of our dreams (which looks different for each of us). I promised that over the next few chapters I would tell you how you could break free of those shackles. And, **I mentioned that we need a model that will work even if you don't have a lot of time to commit to it**.

Furthermore, I suggested **we need a model that will work even if you don't have a lot of money to invest.**

Those are the two issues we're trying to resolve, right?

I believe I've shown you the following:

1. The *best* way to break free of that villain is through network marketing

2. The *best* way to do network marketing is with Young Living Essential Oils

Now, you're at the point of decision— that moment when you choose whether you'll pursue the possibility or not.

Before you decide, I have a three questions for you— all related to whether or not it's worth your pursuit.

Question 1...

If the only thing this opportunity achieves is Secret #1– the only thing it does is positions you to stop trading time for money, to work from anywhere and jump off the hamster wheel– is it worth it?

The answer… is yes!

Question 2…

If the only thing this opportunity accomplishes is Secret #2– if it all it does is empower you to earn while you learn (even if you don't have any experience in this industry and have little to know skills) and move you to a $10,000 / month income or more– it is worth it?

Of course it is!

Question 3…

If the only thing this opportunity achieves is what I showed you in Secret #3– you grow long-term without hassling people to buy stuff they don't want, can't afford, don't know how to use… and will never order again (and, in fact, they come to you begging for more– is it worth it?

Sure. It's worth only that.

I want you to notice, though, that **this opportunity potentially achieves each of those things– and more.** Specifically, this opportunity affords you the chance to escape the 9-5, to live and work from anywhere, to live well, to do the most good, and to bring others on the journey with you.

Last year, the OilyApp team was given the opportunity to interview Sarah, the head of U.S Global Sales for Young Living. Sarah knows the network marketing industry, extremely well, as she once drove a pink Cadillac which she earned as a top-seller with a previous company.

As we interviewed her, she said, "The entry cost to this business is so low. It baffles me that more people don't do it." Then, after a few moments– "When I was working at the other company, people had to invest thousands of dollars to get started. They went to took out loans from their bank, they got second mortgages, they maxed out credit cards…"

(I eluded to this conversation back in chapter 7.)

"What did that do to those people? How did that work out?"

"Well," she said, "because they had to invest so much to get in, they took it seriously. It was almost like the gravity of the big decision– and their financial exposure– motivated them to succeed."

"I guess when the entry cost is higher," one of my business partners– Dr. Jim Bob– continued, "they tend to want to recoup that investment."

"That's true," she replied. "But that huge cost is a barrier that many people have. They *want* to afford it, but they just *can't*."

"I know," Ernie replied. "I tell people how I was against network marketing in the beginning. But, then I tell them that they at least deserve to take a look at what it could possibly achieve for their family."

"Yes," another person added, "but people tend to undervalue the opportunity because the entry cost is to this business is so low. It literally costs more to buy the uniform and shoes to work fast food for minimum wage than it does to launch a biz with a global reach and limitless earning potential."

That said, think about it...

... and think about what it would mean *for you and your family.*

Imagine what life will be like when you're able to...

- To jump off the treadmill
- To work from anywhere
- To live the life of your dreams
- To (permanently) escape the 9-5
- To live well... to be healthy and whole... body, soul, and spirit
- To do the most good– whether it's eliminating debt, jumping off the financial tyranny of surviving paycheck-to-paycheck, helping others, giving to causes you love, or even traveling
- To bring others on the journey with you

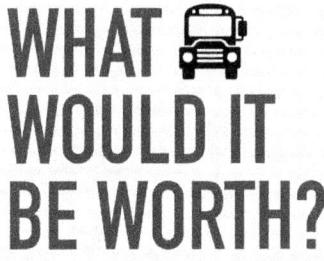

WHAT WOULD IT BE WORTH?

* TO JUMP OFF THE TREADMILL...?
* TO WORK FROM ANYWHERE...?
* TO LIVE THE LIFE OF YOUR DREAMS...?
* TO (PERMANENTLY) ESCAPE THE 9-5...?
* TO LIVE WELL, HEALTHY, WHOLE...?
  (BODY, SOUL, & SPIRIT)
* TO DO THE MOST GOOD...?
  DEBT, SAVE, PAYCHECK-TO-PAYCHECK,
  HELP OTHERS, GIVE, TRAVEL...
* TO BRING OTHERS WITH YOU...?

The irony

Oddly enough, the #1 reason people *don't* get involved isn't because of the money – it's because of time. And it's not that they *don't* have enough time to start now, whereby they could just "fit it in." Rather, they presume they'll (get this) do it *later*. They procrastinate. They see the value and need for the opportunity, they just punt their potential down the field.

Like my friend Bobby.

He phoned me a few years ago as I was heading back from a weekend trip to the beach.

"I've been working 70-hour weeks," he said. "My wife takes the kids on vacation without me, because I can't get away."

He thought he was a Business Owner, the sole proprietor of a landscaping company. But, actually, he was more like Self-Employed. Like the fish and chips guy in chapter 6, he "owned" a business, but *the business really owned him*. If he was away, nothing got done. If he was there, well…he had to do all of the work. It was late Spring, so his busiest season was about to crank up.

"What can I do to help you?" I asked.

"I need to start the home-based business," he said. "We've been using the products for years, but I've got to take the next step and create a way to jump off this treadmill. I'm missing *everything* my family is doing."

He described his daily dilemma of working a bit longer into the evening to provide enough to cover the bills and other basics, versus stopping at a reasonable time in order to go see his wife and two girls.

"I almost did this business last year at this same time," he said. "I knew *then* that I should, *but I didn't*. I would be a year ahead in this process if I'd followed my gut and gotten started."

He asked how much we were making after the first year, so I told him.

"See?" he replied. "I could be that far ahead, but I'm not…"

"Well, better now than never," I said. Then– "A lot of people do what you did. They think it will take too long to truly realize the reality of their dreams. I always tell them– *You're on your own timeline, not anyone else's. And, the time is going to pass anyway. Whether or not you choose to do something with that time– or, rather, what you choose to do with it– is up to you.*"

Almost immediately, he interjected, "Can we catch up tomorrow, face-to-face, and see what I need to do to get going in this?"

"Absolutely."

We set an appointment for the following evening– to meet at a coffee shop, later in the evening. It was well after most people had eaten dinner, yet he had just gotten off work and grabbed a quick shower.

Walking in late, he apologized– "I'm sorry. It was just another one of those days. Every day is like this. That's why I need to make this change."

I outlined the steps it would take. Then, I showed him a picture I snapped of my son, Levi, who was with me that night at the coffee shop.

(Levi has a way of asking me to things and then reminding me that I've already promised to do them.)

"This is a pic I took of Levi when we were on vacation," I said. "We were walking around a store last summer and he brought this to me…"

"That's what I need to show myself," Bobby said. "That picture. That's me."

He begged me to coach him through the process.

I agreed. And, to be honest, it didn't take much convincing. Remember, **in network marketing, you succeed when you help other people succeed. So, empowering him to breakthrough would directly impact his business** *as well as mine*.

He got started.

But then… just two weeks later… *he quit*.

"You OK?" I asked over the phone one evening.

"Yeah. I'm just busy. I think I'm too busy to get started this year. It's a bad time for me. I think it will be better next year."

"I'm not pushing you– or trying to talk you into anything," I told him. After a brief pause, I asked, "But isn't this exactly what you told me a few weeks ago that you did to yourself last year? This means you're going to postpone for *two years* what you thought you should do 365 days ago. Your words, not mine."

"I know," he said. "I'll get around to it someday. I know I will."

Turns out, he hasn't. That convo took place three years ago. He remains stuck working long-hours, trapped in an absolute grind of a the time-for-money tango.

REALITY CHECK

A LOT OF PEOPLE DON'T PURSUE THEIR DREAMS BECAUSE OF THE TIME...

THE TIME IS GOING TO PASS ANYWAY.

MIGHT AS WELL PURSUE THE DREAM WHILE THE TIME DOES...

From Bobby (and dozens of other people who've told me the same story with slightly different details), I learned the following: **the biggest reason people don't "do something" the first time they feel compelled often has nothing to do with the network marketing business model at all.** They eventually see the practical wisdom of it– and how it could work for them. Nor does it have anything to do with the company with which I'm involved or the products we have on hand– they see its recession-proof, easy-to-understand, consumer-friendly nature.

Now, I *thought* their main reasons might be things like–

"I don't have enough time."

(But they all realize that more time is exactly what they're looking for– and that, like we learned in Secret #1, you've got to be Business Owner or Investor in order to make that happen.)

Sometimes, I hear, "I don't have the skill."

THE #1 REASON PEOPLE DON'T GET STARTED

"I CAN DO IT LATER."
LIKE MY FRIEND ROBERT...?
LATER NEVER COMES, RIGHT?
"I'LL CALL YOU THIS TIME NEXT YEAR..."
"PROBABLY SO- LAST YEAR I WAS IN THE EXACT SAME PLACE."

(But most people see the wisdom of Secret #2, and realize they can earn while they learn and learn while they earn– something no other business model or educational pursuit offers.)

Or– "I don't have the money."

(They see the cost to enter this business is super-low. Plus, to enter the market you can spend money on things you were most likely *already* going to purchase that month anyway. In other words, you can just re-direct some of your *already*-budgeted dollars; there's no new outflow. We discussed this in Secret #3).

I've also heard, "Someone else beat me to it."

(I remind them that the market isn't saturated, because the products are consumable. As long as people are alive, they will do certain things every single day. Specifically, people will always take care of themselves.)

Though each of those sound like great reasons for not pursuing the business opportunity, the delay comes down to one super-strange issue.

Here it is. They simply punt their dreams down the field. They procrastinate. **They fail to realize that the future them– the person they are in a year or two years or more– is the exact same person they are today plus the small steps they take each day, regardless of what those steps are**.

I've introduced you to the vehicle.

It's time to begin training– learning and earning concurrently.

The result… is a growing residual income stream. That, and the life you've longed for.

THE VEHICLE
TO YOUR BEST FUTURE

TRAINING
LEARN WHILE YOU EARN

MONEY
GROWING RESIDUAL INCOME

Mini Coopers & Macs

In chapter 7, ("Secret #2 = You Can Earn While You Learn") I showed you an image that stated that one of two things will drive us decisions:

- The reality that we've been created for more than what we're experiencing now, *or*

- The reasons we give not to take steps towards that new reality.

My assumption is that you have some dreams– and that they're worth pursuing.

Sure, you'll hit a few roadblocks and detours along the way. Confront them and continue. After all, **if the time is going to pass anyway, you might as well invest it pursuing that has a payoff.**

A few years ago I bought a Mini Cooper. British racing green, with low profile tires and white racing stripes, the car was outlandishly awesome. Though I hadn't seen too many of them before, as soon as I began whizzing around town in that tiny 5-speed I noticed something odd…

My hometown is full of Mini Coopers.

That same kind of thing happened a few years ago when I made the swap from Windows to Mac. Suddenly, at every bookstore, coffee shop, and park bench I saw hipsters, Gen-Xers, and Boomers alike punching the keys on their Apple devices.

Though Apple has a relatively small marketshare of the market, it seems like theirs are the only computers I saw.

After I made the decision during that Hawaii trip to go "all in" with the business and knew I was going to succeed, my unconscious mind started scanning the environment for evidence that I would. In the same way I suddenly saw the Mini Coopers and Macs that had been present for years, I suddenly saw the opportunity for success that had seemingly eluded me.

Turns out, it had been there all along. I simply needed to decide that this was my time.

What about you?

11. Your Next Step

Now it's time for you to begin your journey. Yes, there is a cost to escaping the time-for-money tango– but *everything* has a cost. The cost of not doing something is greater.

Of course, choosing not to do something is in actuality a decision– it's a choice to stay where you are…

Imagine what life will be like…

- When you wake up ready to face your day!

- When you aren't sluggish at the beginning of your week, but wake up energized and ready to crush it!

- When you look at the bank account and the month is *over* but there's still more money!

You're at a crossroads and can choose one path or the other.

You're one or the other

You're in one of two camps at this point in this book:

- You either already have Young Living essential oils– and are a wholesale member, *or*
- You're not one yet

(Wholesale membership doesn't tie you down to buying something every week for the rest of your life, nor does it sign you up for auto-ship or any other kind of contract… it simply means you get the prices on *the best* products… *and*, unlike Sam's or Costco where you pay a fee to become a member and have the right to shop but don't get any actual products, with Young Living you become a member when you make a purchase.)

If you are a wholesale member, reach out to your direct upline and tell them you would like more information on working "the business side." Most people *don't* work the business– and that's OK. That's what makes the company strong. Young Living isn't just selling a business opportunity; *they sell great products which some people choose to convert to a business opportunity.*

The two best options to become a wholesale member are:

- The Thieves Starter Kit (household products, cleaning, immune support = pictured on top, opposite page), *or*
- The Premium Starter Kit (aka, "essential oils" starter kit = pictured on bottom)

Either way you get the best products on the planet.

You become part of an amazing community, full of people who are learning to walk in health + wholeness. Though we come from a variety of backgrounds, we have this journey in common. And, we support one another and encourage each other through our private Facebook groups.

You'll have access to some of the best resources anywhere. With our regular calls, webinars, and online classes, you'll have great info to continue learning life-changing truths just like you're learning in this book. All of these are free to our team members.

Here's one of the best parts: wholesale members receive a 24% discount on ALL of their purchases AND they're eligible for free products every single month.

Note: if a current member offered you this book, please consult with them.

If no one referred you, or if you took advantage of the online offer for this book, PM or DM @OilyApp on Facebook or Instagram, or call or text 205-291-1391.

12. Links + Resources

The following resources were mentioned during this book:

- The book's webpage = OilyApp.com/Boost

- The Thrift Store video and the download of the chapter from *The Guys' Guide to Oils* that compares network marketing to brick-and-mortar businesses = OilyApp.com/ThriftStore (this was referenced in chapter 4 of this book)

- The business building workshop, *Overflow*, that provides and overview of the entire business opportunity = OilyApp.com/Overflow (this was referenced in chapter 9)

- The Ditch & Switch worksheet (also referenced in chapter 9) = OilyApp.com/ditchNswitch

- The Ditch & Switch book (from chapter 9). Go to OilyApp.com/switch to access the paperback and the video course.

As well, any time we discuss potential incomes we reference Young Living's Income Disclosure Statement. You can locate the most recent edition at the corporate website: YoungLiving.com/IDS

www.ingramcontent.com/pod-product-compliance
Lightning Source LLC
Chambersburg PA
CBHW052354220526
45465CB00003BA/1101